HIDDEN GLORY

HIDDEN GLORY

**The Life and Times of Hampton Plantation
Legend of the South Santee**

by
Mary Bray Wheeler and Genon Hickerson Neblett

Rutledge Hill Press
P.O. Box 140483
Nashville, Tennessee 37214

Published by Rutledge Hill Press, a Thomas Nelson Company, P. O. Box 141000, Nashville, Tennessee 37214.

Typography by ProtoType Graphics, Inc., Nashville, Tennessee

Library of Congress Cataloging-in-Publication Data

Wheeler, Mary Bray, 1942–
    Hidden Glory.
    ISBN 1-55853-859-3 (pbk)
    Bibliography : p.
    Includes Index
    1. Hampton Plantation (S.C.) 2. Rutledge family. 3. South Carolina—Genealogy. 4. South Carolina—Biography. I. Neblett, Genon Hickerson, 1923–joint author. II. Title.
F279.H25W48 1983
975.7'97   83-17618
                                                 CIP

To
the memory of
ARCHIBALD HAMILTON RUTLEDGE
who gave us a "glory" to share
and to
Eleanor Stevenson Rutledge
and
Sue Alston
whose love for Hampton brought life to this
"legend of the South Santee."

Contents

Illustrations

Part V

Part VI

Epilogue

Appendix A

Color Plates

Plate I. Hampton Plantation
Plate II. Charles Cotesworth Pinckney (1746–1825)
Plate III. Thomas Pinckney (1750–1828)
Plate IV. Septima Sexta Middleton Rutledge (1783–1865)
Plate V. Henry Middleton Rutledge (1775–1844)
Plate VI. Aerial view of Middleton Place
Plate VII. Archibald Hamilton Rutledge (1883–1973)

End Sheet

With the walnut-framed picture of her beloved husband Prince always near, Sue recalls the glory of that "great day in Hampton" that is now the legend of the South Santee.

Study of Sue Alston, "Guardian Angel of Hampton Plantation."
Artist—Larry Martin
Wren's Nest Gallery
Jacksonville, Alabama

South Carolina Yellow Jessamine
Designed for **Hidden Glory** *by*
Larry Martin and Crystal Hancock
Wren's Nest Gallery—Jacksonville, Alabama

Acknowledgments

Hidden Glory actually began with the years of research for *Chosen Exile*, our biography of Septima Sexta Middleton Rutledge and any acknowledgment must first include all those who were a part of that effort, especially the Rutledge Company of Gadsden, Alabama, Colonel and Mrs. Clarence W. Daugette, Jr., and Marcella Lawley. Their continued interest has encouraged us and for that we are grateful.

Our South Carolina ties have been strong and the cooperation of the staff at Middleton Place Foundation has been invaluable. Sarah Lytle, director, and Barbara Doyle, editor of the *Middleton Place Notebook*, have consistently aided us and made each research trip a special event. Barbara Smith and Elise Pinckney have provided insights to family connections and have shared our excitement. Thank you to all those connected with Hampton Plantation: Bob Mitchell; Will, Samuel, and Sue Alston; the South Carolina Department of Parks, Recreation, and Tourism, State Parks division; Judge and Mrs. Irvine Hart Rutledge; and especially our cherished friend, Eleanor Rutledge, who introduced us to Sue Alston and inspired us to write *Hidden Glory*.

Those involved with the production and development of a manuscript into a finished work deserve our most grateful acknowledgment:

For editorial assistance; Alice C. Ewing and Sandra W. Fribley.

For typing; Margaret Hogshead.

For proofreading; Alice and James Ewing.

For photography; Charles Gay, William T. Justice, R. Alan Powell, Leslie Pritikin, C.E. Staton, Jr., Silvia Sullivan, and Jim Wheeler—credits appear with individual illustrations.

For typography; ProtoType Graphics—John and Carol Adams, Ken Callaway, Linda Gann, Jeralyn Johnson, Tod Missick, and Jeannie Northcott.

For kind permission to use quotations from manuscripts, letters, or taped interviews; Middleton Place Foundation, Historical Society of Pennsylvania, Kentucky Library—Western Kentucky University, South Carolina Historical Society, *South Carolina Historical Magazine*, South Caroliniana Library (Archibald Rutledge Collection)—University of South Carolina, Tennessee Historical Society, Sue Alston, W.G. Hutchison, Elise Pinckney, Eleanor Stevenson Rutledge, Irvine Hart Rutledge, and Margaret Hamilton Seabrook.

For permission to use art; the Wren's Nest Gallery—Larry Martin and Crystal Hancock.

For loyal support and encouragement; Betsy Collins, Tom Dority, Saye and Grady Fleming, Dot and Ed Hickerson, Evelyn O'Lee, Millie Price, and Marilisa Wheeler.

A personal word of gratitude to our publishers, Ron Pitkin and Larry Stone, for their faith in us; to Joyce Blackburn and Eugenia Price for their encouragement and sharing as they taught us the art of biography; to Faith Hickerson Dycus and Ray Neblett for their travels with us and for their genuine enthusiasm for our work; to Shannon and Jimmy Wheeler for cheerfully making it through *another* book; to Alice and James Ewing and Margie Hogshead, whose diligent efforts kept us on schedule; and to all those with individual acknowledgments that appear in Appendix A, in the Resources, and with the illustrations.

To our families, to each person who shared this time with us, and to our readers we extend our love and join Archibald Rutledge in saying "may your life illumined be by dreams of Hampton in your heart."

Mary Bray Wheeler and Genon Hickerson Neblett
September 1983

Preface

"A great day in Hampton!" We would hear that phrase many times in the months to come, but for now we could not know the significance of those words. For us, it was enough, that memorable days were coming, closer together than we ever thought or dreamed possible.

It was Monday, June 30, 1980. Just the day before we had been guests of honor at Middleton Place House and Gardens near Charleston, South Carolina. The occasion—Arthur Middleton's 238th birthday and the premier autograph party for *Chosen Exile,* our biography of Septima Sexta Middleton Rutledge, Arthur's seventh child, sixth daughter. That was not a *hard* act to follow—*impossible* would have been the more accurate descriptive adjective. Yet here we were—family and friends—on the morning after, extending our celebration with a long-awaited visit to the place Archibald Rutledge, late South Carolina poet laureate, had called his *Home by the River.* Our guide, his daughter-in-law Eleanor Stevenson Rutledge (also a direct descendant of Septima), had been hostess at Hampton for over twenty-five years and had traveled from her home in Jacksonville, Alabama, for the festivities at Middleton Place. Her assistance with *Chosen Exile* had been of utmost value to us, and she knew how very much we wanted to see Hampton.

An impressive caravan of cars from Alabama, Georgia, Tennessee, and North and South Carolina joined ours, traveling north from Charleston along U.S. Highway 17. Just before reaching the South Santee River, we turned west, crossed the King's Highway used by George Washington in 1791, and entered the drive to Hampton. Hidden from view until the very last moment, the great Rutledge manor house, begun in 1730, finally stood before us, bravely, silently bearing the indignities of restoration.

We should have been beyond tears. Emotion-filled events had commenced on Saturday as we had watched descendants of Septima and Henry Rutledge meet for the first time. There were tears then, and there were tears as we were escorted across the lawn at Middleton Place on Sunday and saw, seated under the oaks, those members (very precious by now) of our "family of the heart." This was followed by more tears, not to mention a genuine sob or two, as we faced twenty-two of our own dearest friends and relatives who could not bear to miss such a grand occasion. Now it was Monday, and we wept again.

Strangely enough, we felt as if we had been to Hampton before; yet our "homecoming" was coupled with a great sense of loss at never knowing the man who had loved Hampton best. We always knew there would be another book, and this was the day we exchanged tearful smiles and the secret knowledge—our hidden glory—that it would be about Hampton.

In researching *Chosen Exile* we uncovered a multitude of connectional stories. From the time *Chosen Exile* was published in 1980 and we had spent our first "great day in Hampton," we jealously guarded every index card, scratch pad, and notebook with the premeditated intention of completing a trilogy about our beloved family of the heart. This second work, *Hidden Glory*, has been once again an adventure, a labor of love, and a sharing of all we have found to be the most informative about our subject, Hampton Plantation.

Hidden Glory is a biography as was *Chosen Exile*. Both books tell the story of a life. *Hidden Glory* reveals the life and times of a plantation house, now over 250 years old. Human lifespan rarely exceeds one century; therefore this biography necessarily includes generations of owners and occupants in order to acquaint the reader with the main character, Hampton Plantation.

Nothing intrigued us more than the items of correspondence, innocently penned long years ago, which served to sharpen our perception of those very real people of Hampton. Nowhere could we find a more vivid description of this "home by the river" than in the words of its last owner, Archibald Rutledge.

Yet there was one exception—the single most fascinating view of Hampton came to us through eyes that could then see only "the shadow of my finger." The mind and voice of Hampton's centenarian-plus "guardian angel," Sue Alston, still paint a picture "noble and bright" for any who will listen. And listen we must—those letters, diaries, and poems; the conversations with Archibald's son, Irvine, and his daughter-in-law, Eleanor; the spoken memories of Sue Alston—all those voices of the past and the present tell us that the plantation house itself, this majestic, columned structure now concealed by dense undergrowth, is only a reminder of Hampton's hidden glory. The spot of light unseen is the legend of the South Santee: the Hampton that dwelt within the souls of those who lived there. They still speak to us in poetic whispers of that "great day in Hampton"—a day we may envision only if we listen with our hearts, else the glory be forever hidden.

HIDDEN GLORY

Part I

THE OWNER

Daniel Huger Horry (1738–1785)

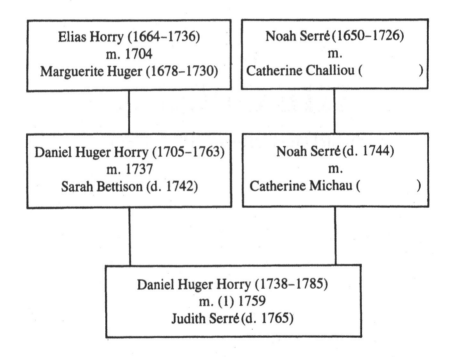

| Elias Horry (1664–1736)
m. 1704
Marguerite Huger (1678–1730) | Noah Serré (1650–1726)
m.
Catherine Challiou (   ) |
| Daniel Huger Horry (1705–1763)
m. 1737
Sarah Bettison (d. 1742) | Noah Serré (d. 1744)
m.
Catherine Michau (   ) |

Daniel Huger Horry (1738–1785)
m. (1) 1759
Judith Serré (d. 1765)

Genealogy I—The Owner
Daniel Huger Horry
(1738–1785)

Chapter 1

Hampton Plantation, on the South Santee, stands as a guardian of her own mysteries. Careful study, precise documentation, and even family legends have failed to produce any recorded evidence as to the positive identity of Hampton's earliest builder or the exact date of construction. Two theories of dating the original section have been advanced, and most historians would agree that it may be valid to consider either possibility, but neither is entirely plausible. Whether or not an early builder emerges from the dusty records remains a minor consideration in view of the important place Hampton Plantation occupies in any historical interpretation of the Huguenot development along the Santee delta. The Protestant emigrants from France brought a rich cultural influence into a wild, steamy, unsettled Carolina of the late seventeenth century. Northern Europe provided no comparison for acclimation to this tropical wilderness with its heat variations, hurricanes, wildlife, insects, dreaded fever, and soon-to-be-extinct Sewee Indian population.

Long called the French Santee, the mighty Santee River begins not far from Columbia, South Carolina, where the Wateree and Congaree rivers unite. Sixty miles from its mouth the Santee divides, forming two streams that flow independently into the Atlantic Ocean. Between the North and South Santee a lonely delta forms and is one to three miles wide throughout its length. It was along the creeks and bluffs of this delta that the Huguenot settlers found the freedom as well as the potential for the agricultural prosperity which they sought.

The Carolina Territory was originally a land grant issued by Charles II of England in 1663 to a small group of Lords Proprietors who came by way of Barbados and founded a small settlement in 1670 near the coast on the west bank of what is now known as the Ashley River. At the direction of Lord Anthony Ashley-Cooper in 1680 the townsite was moved across the river to Oyster Point where two rivers, now the Ashley and the Cooper, join to flow into the Atlantic Ocean. It was eight blocks in size, amply fortified, and appropriately named Charles Town. An increase in population caused the first extension of the boundaries in 1717. The riverfront areas along the Cooper became important because of shipping needs and therefore were the first to experience heavy development and further changes in the town's boundaries.

Just prior to the relocation of Charles Town, Protestants from France were given the right to join the colony. On October 24, 1679, King Charles II provided not only a grant for these Huguenots to settle in Carolina but extended each immigrant free passage, seventy acres of land, and the added inducement of acreage for each servant brought to the colony. This grant predated the Edict of Nantes, which forced most French Protestants to the British colonies. In 1680 Noah Serré was among the first fifty Huguenot settlers to arrive in Carolina. In 1694 he purchased a lot in Charles Town with money he had earned there as a weaver and soon was given citizenship rights equal to the English crafts-men of the area. By 1699 he had decided that he and his son Noah should purchase land along the Santee River in St. James Parish; they, along with more than one hundred other French immigrants, made the transi-tion from villager to plantation owner. However, it was not uncommon for the more affluent colonists in the region, both then and later, to enjoy the convenience of keeping both their town houses and their more dis-persed and isolated dwellings on the various plantations which thrived with the introduction of rice and indigo along with the production of forest products such as tar and pitch. By 1726, the year he prepared his will, Noah Serré had acquired considerable wealth. Noah, Jr., was per-haps forty-five years old when his father died, and because of his inheri-tance he became the most prominent of the Santee inhabitants. He was active in community affairs and those of his church, the original "Church of Geneva" Huguenot congregation on the Santee. It had been established in the midst of the French plantations and the dwindling Se-wee Indian population but the poor location and natural disasters had caused this first Huguenot community, Jamestown, to cease to exist by 1720. The Anglican parish of St. James Santee in Craven County re-placed it. This Anglican church parish was the unit of local government from 1706 until the 1778 constitution endorsed the principle of separa-tion of church and state.

At his death in 1744 Noah, Jr., owned 120 slaves, much valuable property in Charles Town, and a number of large plantations. He and his wife, Catherine, had five daughters and one son, Noah III, all of whom were minors at the time of Noah, Jr.'s, death. When Noah III died in 1752, his sisters Catherine, Mary, Judith, Elizabeth, and Hester divided the Serré estate among themselves. Popular legend (since the early part of this century) has indicated that Judith received the Santee plantation land holdings. However, there is in fact no indication that her portion was near Wambaw Creek where Hampton stands today. It is only known that her husband, Daniel Horry, was an executor of her father's will. Daniel's grandparents, Elias and Marguerite Huger Horry, were also prominent Huguenot immigrants whose Santee land holdings did include the area along Wambaw Creek.

The mystery seems to be whether the earliest portion of Hampton was constructed prior to 1730 by Noah Serré or whether one of the Horry plantation owners (Elias, his son Daniel Huger, or his grandson Daniel Huger, Jr.,) built the original structure. Daniel Huger Horry, Jr., did acquire Judith Serré's land following her death and that of their two children prior to 1767, as well as five thousand acres of Horry land on Wambaw Creek when his father died in 1763. It is without question that the present house evolved from a simply built dwelling with four rooms on the first floor and two on the floor above. The two chimney columns, with fireplaces, did not extend into the basement area. Sometime before 1785 the east and west wings and two additional fireplaces were added as well as two more rooms on the second floor. There is also structural evidence that the main stairwell was altered and that the front entrance was to the south even before the addition of the portico, traditionally dated just prior to 1791.

Whatever the origin of Hampton's structure, there is no doubt of its existence nor of its sole ownership by Daniel Huger Horry, Jr., at the time of his marriage to Harriott Pinckney in 1768. Following his death in 1785, the inventory of Hampton listed furniture for twelve rooms—the same number in the Hampton of today. This home of Daniel and Harriott Horry was indeed the showplace of the Santee.

Part II

THE HOSTESS

Harriott Pinckney [Horry] (1748–1830)

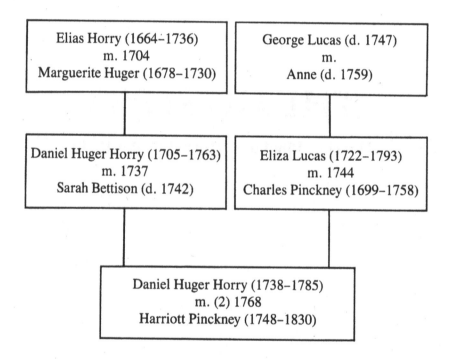

Elias Horry (1664–1736) m. 1704 Marguerite Huger (1678–1730)	George Lucas (d. 1747) m. Anne (d. 1759)
Daniel Huger Horry (1705–1763) m. 1737 Sarah Bettison (d. 1742)	Eliza Lucas (1722–1793) m. 1744 Charles Pinckney (1699–1758)

Daniel Huger Horry (1738–1785)
m. (2) 1768
Harriott Pinckney (1748–1830)

Genealogy II—The Hostess
Harriott Pinckney [Horry]
(1748–1830)

Chapter 2

With the marriage in 1768 of Daniel Huger Horry, Jr., to Harriott Pinckney, one of the wealthiest political families in the Royal Province of Carolina became forever linked with Hampton Plantation. Harriott's parents, Charles and Eliza Lucas Pinckney were very much a part of the early settlement of Charles Town and South Carolina, as the territory was called after 1729.

At age fifteen, Eliza Lucas migrated to South Carolina from Antigua with her parents, George and Anne Lucas. Her younger sister, Polly, came with them in 1738 to a plantation on Wappoo Creek seventeen miles from Charles Town. Eliza's grandfather, John Lucas, originally from Essex, England, had been a successful sugar planter on Antigua Island and left his son George three plantations in South Carolina (Wappoo, Waccamaw, and Garden Hill on the Combahee River). This vast inheritance gave George Lucas not only an opportunity for financial gain but also the ability to provide an increased atmosphere of physical safety for his family. These factors prompted the relocation of the Lucas family to Wappoo Plantation.

By spring of 1739, George Lucas, at that time a major in the British Army, was ordered to return to active duty in Antigua. War with Spain was imminent, and upon his departure for extended military command, sixteen-year-old Eliza was left to manage the three South Carolina plantations. Her responsibilities included supervision of six hundred-acre Wappoo, fifteen-hundred acre Combahee, which mainly produced forest products and salt pork, and the task of directing the overseers of their three-thousand-acre rice field parcels along the Waccamaw River. In addition, Eliza cared for her semi-invalid mother, tutored young Polly, and gave elementary instructions to the slave children at Wappoo. These tasks alone were monumental, and yet her keen interest in cultivation prompted this amazing young woman to experiment successfully with the tiny black indigo seeds her father sent from the British West Indies. In 1741, after several setbacks, Eliza produced a small crop of indigo, which in the years to follow substantially increased export profit for South Carolina planters.

Eliza's interests were varied and her love of learning made her an apt student of literature, music, and even the law. She spent many hours with

Charles and Elizabeth Lamb Pinckney at Belmont Plantation on the Cooper River. Charles Pinckney's father Thomas was born in 1666 in the town of Bishop Auckland, County Durham, in the north of England. Thomas came to Carolina in April 1692 and there married Grace Bedon who died about a year later leaving no issue. When Thomas returned to England due to the deaths of his parents and eldest brother, he met Mary Cotesworth, daughter of sixty-eight-year-old Charles Cotesworth. They were married, moved to Charles Town, and there had three sons— Thomas, Charles, and William. Charles, who had been named for Mary Cotesworth's father, studied in London and was the first native South Carolinian to receive full professional legal training. He married Elizabeth Lamb in England and they returned to Charles Town in December 1727. He was admitted to the bar, entered the Commons House of the General Assembly, and by 1734 was one of the most prosperous attorneys in South Carolina. As Mrs. Pinckney's health grew exceedingly frail, the older Pinckney couple found pleasure in the company of their accomplished young friend, Eliza Lucas. Charles Pinckney encouraged Eliza in her studies and shared his library with her.

In 1742 Eliza's father was promoted to lieutenant colonel and soon after was appointed lieutenant governor of Antigua. In December 1743 he sent his son, Ensign George Lucas, to South Carolina with the task of bringing the rest of the Lucas family back to Antiqua to be with him. They all returned except Eliza. Not long after the death of her friend, Elizabeth Lamb Pinckney, in January 1744, she consented to become the second wife of Charles Pinckney. Upon learning of Eliza's plans to leave Carolina for Antigua, the newly widowed Mr. Pinckney had proposed to Eliza and had written her father for his approval. After receiving the long-awaited answer, Eliza Lucas and Charles Pinckney were married on May 27, 1744, in St. Andrew's parish. They stayed at Wappoo until the Lucas family departed for the West Indies on July 2 of that same year. Then Charles Pinckney rented Wappoo to a tenant, but retained rights to the valuable stand of indigo that had been part of Eliza's dowry. The Pinckneys then established Belmont Plantation as their home while Charles supervised the design and building of a grand town house for his young wife. The mansion was on East Bay overlooking the Charles Town harbor.

In the following years Eliza and Charles had four children: Charles Cotesworth (b. December 11, 1746); George Lucas (b. June 14, 1747– d. June 19, 1747); Harriott (b. August 7, 1748); and Thomas (b. October 23, 1750).

Grief over the premature birth and death of her second son added to the shock and sadness Eliza already bore from news of her father's death. Lieutenant Colonel George Lucas had been taken prisoner by the French while traveling from Antigua to England. His death had been kept from Eliza, but she accidentally discovered a letter containing the details.

On September 22, 1752, James Glen, royal governor of South Carolina, appointed Charles Pinckney chief justice and swore him in the same day. In March, Pinckney learned that his position had not been confirmed by the Crown and that Peter Leigh, high bailiff of Westminster, London, was being appointed to the highest judicial post in Carolina. Disheartened by this reversal, Charles Pinckney took his wife and children to England where they remained nearly five years. Pinckney was received as special agent to His Majesty's Council for South Carolina, and Eliza enjoyed her time in London as the wife of a representative to the Crown. By May 1758, Charles Pinckney had decided to return to Carolina to set his affairs in order. Management had been left with his brother, William, who had since suffered a stroke and was unable to supervise the large land holdings in a satisfactory manner. The Pinckney sons, Charles Cotesworth, twelve years old, and Thomas, seven-and-one-half years old, were left in Camberwell-on-the-Thames at a small school run by a Mr. Gerrard. Their nine-year-old sister Harriott returned with her parents to South Carolina. While Charles Pinckney toured his plantations, distraught over their neglected condition, he fell victim to "country fever" (malaria) and within three weeks, on July 12, 1758, was dead. He was buried in St. Philip's churchyard. Once again left with enormous responsibility, Eliza Lucas Pinckney was doubly grief stricken by this unexpected loss and by being separated from her sons. It was the next month before she was able to write to them:

August 1758

To My dear Children Charles and Thomas Pinckney

How shall I write to you! What shall I say to you! My dear, my ever dear Children! but if possible more so now than Ever, for I have a tale to tell you that will peirce your tender infant hearts! You have mett with the greatest loss, my children, you could meet with upon Earth! Your dear, dear father, the best and most valueable of parents, is no more!

God Almighty soport your tender minds in this terrible distress, and enable you to put your whole trust and confidence in Him, enable you to rely on him that he will be your father, your comfort, and soport. Endeavour to submit to the Will of God in the best manner you can, and let it be a comfort to you, my dear babes, as long as you live that you had such a father! He has set you a great and good example. May the Lord enable you both to follow it, and may God Almighty fulfill all your pius fathers prayers upon both your heads. They were almost incessant for blessings both spiritual and temporal on you both. He never mentioned you but with repeated blessings, and with up lifted Eyes and hands to heaven; God bless them, God bless them was his constant prayer when ever he named you, and that was very often....he and we are indebted to the infinitely wise and good God, and above all for the most comfortable and joyous hope that we shall meet in Glory never never more to be separated!

This hope, This expectation, is the soport and comfort of my life, a life which I will endeavour as much as is in my power to preserve, not only as a duty to the God that gave it, but as a duty from me to the remains of your dear dear father, to you and your dear Sister; and I hope the Almighty will enable me to do my duty in every instance by you, and that all my future life may be spent to do you good, and in showing to you, the dear pledges of the sincerest affection that ever was upon Earth, how much, how truly, I loved and honoured Your dear father by my affection and care of you.

Adieu, my beloved children! God Almighty bless, guide and protect you! Make you his own children, and worthy such a father as yours was, and comfort you in this great affliction is the fervent and constant prayer of Your ever affectionate tho' greatly afflicted Mother

Eliza. Pinckney

who feels most exquisitely for you what you must suffer upon the receit of this letter. God Almighty soport your tender spirrits.

Amen.Amen.

She did not see her sons again until Charles Cotesworth was twenty-three and Thomas was twenty-two. The Pinckney land holdings in 1758, which Eliza supervised, included: Belmont Plantation; the island group (now called Pinckney Island); one-thousand-acre Auckland Plantation on the Ashepoo River; Pinckney Plains Plantation, west of the upper Ashley River; Marshlands Plantation on the Cooper River; five hundred acres on the Savannah River; and five hundred acres at Four Holes. There were two homes on East Bay and other property near Colleton Square in Charles Town. A large portion of the profit from the Pinckney plantations went toward the fulfilling of instructions left by Charles Pinckney in his will for securing educations for his two sons.

Harriott Pinckney spent the ten years following her father's death ably helping her mother manage the Pinckney plantations and property in Charles Town. Her name appears with her mother's as renting a pew in St. Michael's church in Charles Town. Those additions to the pew rental list of December 1, 1760, resemble a social register: Pew 41, Peter Manigault; Pew 45, William Blake; Pew 46, John McQueen; Pew 49, William Middleton; Pew 60, Henry Middleton; Pew 61, Thomas Middleton; Pew 62, Thomas Shubrick; Pew 64, Daniel Ravenel, Jr,; Pew 73, Eliza Pinckney—Harriott Pinckney; Pew 78, Daniel Horry; and Pew 107, Daniel Blake.

Harriott Pinckney was a scholarly young lady who spoke fluent French and attracted many suitors, yet she adhered to her mother's wish that she not marry young. But in time she was courted by widower and wealthy Santee rice planter, Daniel Horry, and Eliza Pinckney was pleased at the prospect of her daughter's union with this native Carolinian who earlier had studied law at the Inner Temple and had been called to the English Bar. She considered his Huguenot heritage a fine complement to the Pinckney line in America as well as to Harriott's own educational and cultural background in England, so she gave her blessing to their romance, and Harriott and Daniel were married on February 15, 1768. The couple divided their time between Hampton Plantation and Daniel's large manor house at the corner of Broad and Legare streets in Charles Town. Harriott Pinckney Horry was highly accomplished in the skills she would need as mistress of a large plantation and as hostess to gatherings of the most prominent citizens of mid-eighteenth-century Charles Town.

Chapter 3

Although married life at Hampton Plantation for Harriott and Daniel Horry began during an era of unrest for South Carolina, social activities in the early 1770s did not reflect the dramatic undercurrent of political upheaval that would soon engulf townspeople and planters alike. Of particular interest to Daniel Horry and his brother-in-law, Charles Cotesworth Pinckney, were the races held each February in Charles Town. At that time folks from throughout the colony gathered for a week of festivities. Young Pinckney, a bachelor and newly commissioned to practice before the bar of South Carolina, enjoyed the dances as well as the races. He participated in the events and showed keen interest in the placing of Daniel Horry's horses. It is known that Harriott did not share the men's enthusiasm for horses and would have preferred fine rows of trees at Hampton rather than open tracks reserved for Daniel's horses. Family gatherings at Hampton were frequent during this period, and Harriott's mother, Eliza Pinckney, was more and more a part of that household. The records kept in Daniel Horry's Bible tell of the close association of the family with each other and with the church.

THE HOLY BIBLE

Containing the Old and New Testaments:
Newly Translated out of the Original Tongues;
And with the former TRANSLATIONS
Diligently Compared and Revised.
By His Majesties Special Command.
Appointed to be Read in Churches.
Printed in the Year, MDCCXV.

Dan Horry, married Miss Harriott Pinckney./Daughter of the Hon. Ch: Pinckney Esq:/this 15th day of February 1768.—by the Rev:ᵈ M:ʳRob:ʳ Smith Rector for the Parish of S:ᵗ Phillip Ch:ˢ Town. S.º Carolina./
Daniel the son of Daniel & Harriott Horry, was Born 13:ᵗʰ August 1769. on a Sunday between the Hours of four & five in the afternoon.—and was Baptised by the Rever:ᵈ M:ʳ Hart—assistant to the Parish of S:ᵗ Mich:ˡ Ch:ˢ Town/by Private Baptism/the 25:ᵗʰ August 1769.—/—

Harriott Pinckney, the Daughter of Dan & Harriott Horry was Born the 4th day of October 1770 on a Sunday between the Hours of 10 & 11 o'clock in the forenoon . . . And was Baptised by the Rev:^{d} M:^{r} Lewis Rector for the parish of S:^{t} Pauls, on Friday the 27:th Novemb: 1770. at S:^{t} Phillips Church Ch: Town. Her God-Mothers Right Honble Lady Mary Middleton, & M:^{rs} Sarah Pinckney—& her God Father Tho:^{s} Pinckney Esqr—

On the same day was received at Church Daniel our first Born His God Fathers Charles Cotesworth Pinckney esq.^{r} & Thomas Cousans Esqr (of the Island Jamaica) His God-Mother Mrs Eliza Pinckney.

Just as the prosperous Horry couple heralded the births of their only two children, a son, Daniel (b. August 13, 1769), followed by a daughter, Harriott Pinckney (b. October 4, 1770), the American colonies began experiencing the first in a series of what came to be known as the Intolerable Acts. These were measures taken by the British Parliament designed to make examples of those colonies actively showing opposition to taxation. On December 3, 1773, Charles Town's new Exchange Building was the scene of a mass rally protesting the British tax on tea. The East India Company had a cargo of 257 chests of tea in Charles Town harbor that December night. Debate ensued as to the disposal of the shipment so as to avoid taxation. Since the present government of South Carolina traces its beginnings to this anti-tea rally, it has particular historical significance. Subsequent meetings of this group eventually evolved into the General Committee, the several Provincial Congresses, and finally into the state General Assembly. The citizens meeting that December resolved not to receive the shipment of tea. The patriots, nevertheless, were surprised by customs officers who moved the chests of tea into the Exchange warehouse. Despite this action, the colonists kept the situation in hand by locking the doors to the warehouse. South Carolina was the only colony to handle the East India Tea Company in this manner. In Philadelphia and in New York the merchants were forced to sail back to England with their full loads, while in Boston, on the evening of December 16, the entire consignment was thrown overboard during the now-famous "Boston Tea Party." Significantly, the entire Charles Town shipment remained locked away until 1776 when it was sold to provide funds for the defense of South Carolina against the British.

In June 1774 a committee of Charles Town gentlemen organized a massive fund raising effort to aid the citizens of Boston whose port had been closed since the previous March. Daniel Horry was among those who volunteered to collect donations. Although South Carolina was one of the last colonies to learn of the distress in New England, their response in money and supplies was the first received and far exceeded any other contributions.

From the beginning, the South Carolina patriots assumed leadership in innovative ways toward liberating the American colonies from British tyranny. The family names connected with Hampton Plantation became linked indelibly to the stirrings of unrest in South Carolina, to the decision-making in their native assemblies, and to the eventual turning of the tide toward independence for the American colonies.

Daniel Horry joined the political arena early in the struggle for colonial rights. In 1775 he was a member of the First Provincial Congress. He was appointed to the 1775 Congressional Committee of Intelligence and in September returned to serve in the Second Provincial Congress. His brother, Peter Horry, and his brother-in-law, Charles Cotesworth Pinckney, also were members of South Carolina's Provincial Congresses. Thomas Pinckney, Daniel's other brother-in-law, received his call to the English bar on November 25, 1774, and by December had returned to Charles Town. Thomas had been anxious to leave England so that he could be with his family and yet he had been obligated to complete his requirements for the bar in compliance with his late father's will. Both of Charles Pinckney's sons were now practicing attorneys in Charles Town just as Charles Pinckney had wished. Little did the elder Pinckney realize, however, that his sons and son-in-law would become outspoken participants in a rebellion against the Crown, just as none of these men could have foretold the far-reaching effects their actions would have on their families and property.

Chapter 4

As South Carolina entered the cause for independence by a radical break with King George III and the British Parliament, union with the other twelve colonies was their only recourse. To some it may have appeared out of character for South Carolina to reverse allegiance and to end long-cherished traditions. Yet by 1776 Carolinians firmly believed that the policies of the British government threatened their very rights as Englishmen. To declare independence was no easy course of action, for ties with the mother country were economic and social as well as familial, and emotion-packed debates accompanied every decision for a permanent separation. Tension throughout the decade prior to the Revolution was linked with uncomfortable situations of divided loyalties. South Carolina's native lieutenant governor, William Bull, was well loved and respected, whereas the royal governor, Lord Charles Greville Montagu, attempted to defeat and discourage representation at each session of the Assembly. He even changed the location of the government from Charles Town to Beaufort for their meeting, October 8, 1772, in order to make attendance for the autumn session as difficult as possible. His high-handed efforts failed and only served to inflame the patriots and incite their reactions. He was followed, in June of 1775, by Lord William Campbell, whose commission as royal governor was greeted with sullen silence in Charles Town.

In July 1774, at a general meeting held in Charles Town, five men were elected to represent South Carolina at a general congress in Philadelphia that fall. They were Henry Middleton, John Rutledge, Thomas Lynch, Christopher Gadsden, and Edward Rutledge. On October 22, 1774, Henry Middleton of the South Carolina delegation was elected president of this First Continental Congress following the resignation of Virginia's Peyton Randolph. This body agreed to the nonimportation movement, which would cut off exports to Great Britain within one year, as an attempt to pressure Parliament into a repeal of its objectionable taxes. The five delegates reported to South Carolina's First Provincial Congress in January 1775 and remained hopeful that the measures outlined by the Continental Congress would be successful. The South Carolina Congress voted to send the same five men to Philadelphia in May 1775, for the Second Continental Congress.

The actions taken by the colonials were not well received by Parliament, and there seemed to be no peaceful solution to the conflict with England. On April 19, 1775, skirmishes between British regular troops and New England minutemen at Lexington and Concord marked the beginning of the Revolutionary War. Within two months South Carolina raised three regiments, two of light infantry and one of mounted rangers, which eventually became part of the Continental army. Officers for the regiments were chosen by ballots cast by the Provincial Congress. In the ranking of captains Charles Cotesworth Pinckney was first (140 votes), Daniel Horry, sixth (131 votes), and Thomas Pinckney, fourteenth (98 votes). Military matters moved briskly, and September 15 proved a strategic date in the history of South Carolina, as provincial troops captured Fort Johnson, the royal stronghold on James Island guarding Charles Town harbor, and the government passed completely into the hands of the patriots.

The military involvement of Harriott Pinckney Horry's husband and brothers greatly affected her and her mother in the years to follow. Harriott wrote a friend in Georgetown, just north of Hampton:

> ...I think dejection appears at present, the Cloud that hangs over us, ready to burst upon our heads, calls for all our Fortitude to meet the awful event with that decency and resignation becoming a Xtian....Almost all the Women and many hundred Men have left Town....My brother is at ye Fort. Tom at present recruiting. Mr. Horry goes to ye Fort tomorrow to spend a month.

As the men of the family were fighting the British, an ever-increasing population of women and children sought sanctuary at Hampton Plantation because of the security of its relatively isolated location. Among these were Harriott's sister-in-law, Sally Pinckney; Sally's sister Hester (Mrs. Charles Drayton); another sister Henrietta (Mrs. Edward Rutledge); their sister-in-law Mary Izard (Mrs. Arthur Middleton); and many of their children.

In 1773, Charles Cotesworth Pinckney, twenty-seven at the time, married seventeen-year-old Sarah [Sally] Middleton, daughter of Henry and the late Mary Williams Middleton. Henry Middleton's grandfather, Edward, came to the Carolinas by way of Barbados in 1678 and was Lords Proprietor deputy. Edward's estate, The Oaks, was a group of large land grants in the Parish of St. James Goose Creek. Edward's son, Arthur, was president of the 1719 Colonial Convention and at the time of

Photo—R. Alan Powell
Courtesy—Middleton Place
Foundation, Charleston, South
Carolina.

Henry Middleton
(1717–1784).

Photo—R. Alan Powell
Courtesy—Middleton Place Foundation, Charleston, South Carolina.

Known today as Middleton Place House, the south wing and a matching north wing were added to the original house by Henry Middleton (1717–1784) in 1755. This portion escaped destruction by Union forces and was remodeled to serve as the Middleton's family residence by 1870.

his death in 1739 was able to leave his son, Henry, vast land holdings in Carolina, Barbados, and England.

It was this Henry Middleton who married Mary, the only daughter and heiress of John Williams in 1741. Mary Williams brought to the marriage a considerable dowry, which included an estate on the Ashley River that she and Henry named Middleton Place. From this country seat, which boasted the first formal gardens in America, Henry maintained a position of wealth and political influence. He was Speaker of the Commons, Commissioner of Indian Affairs, and a member of the Governor's Council (a position he resigned in 1770 to take leadership in the opposition to the British Parliament). When he became president of the First Continental Congress, he owned fifty thousand acres of land and some eight hundred slaves. During the Revolution Henry personally contributed 210,000 pounds currency in six separate loans to the state without ever redeeming the principal or the interest, making him the seventh largest bondholder.

Henry and Mary Williams Middleton had five sons and seven daughters, several of whom figured prominently in the story of the Revolution and were a significant part of the family history of Hampton Plantation. Following Mary Williams Middleton's death in 1761, Henry was married for ten years to Maria Henrietta, youngest daughter of South Carolina's beloved governor, William Bull. She died without heirs in March 1772. His third wife, Lady Mary Mackenzie Ainslie, daughter of the third Earl of Cromartie, also sought refuge at Hampton during the war with her step-daughters.

Meanwhile the makeup of South Carolina's representation in the Continental Congress was changing. Illness prevented Henry Middleton's return in 1776, and his less conservative son, Arthur, succeeded him there, along with Henry's son-in-law, Edward Rutledge, who succeeded his older brother, John Rutledge. Thomas Heyward, Jr., replaced Christopher Gadsden and Thomas Lynch, Jr., succeeded his own father. These were all friends, neighbors, or family connections to the women at Hampton Plantation. The Lynch family lived at Hopsewee on the North Santee, a neighboring plantation to Hampton. The Heywards were successful cotton planters from St. Luke's Parish and Christopher Gadsden, a distinguished merchant of Charles Town. Their ties were of friendship with those gathered at Hampton though they remained in town.

The Middleton/Rutledge/Pinckney connection was a bond of friendship as well as blood which irreversibly linked Charles Town, Middleton

Place, and Hampton Plantation to the future security and, indeed, the very existence of South Carolina and the soon-to-be free nation of America.

John and Edward Rutledge were the sons of Dr. John Rutledge who had immigrated to South Carolina in 1735 from County Tyrone, Ireland (Ulster).

Dr. John's family centered their activity around Christ Church Parish near Charles Town, where he was vestryman in 1746, and along with his brother, Andrew, was a member of Christ Church General Assembly. The two brothers were members of the Charles Town Library Society in 1750. John served as surgeon in the Charles Town Militia in the fight against the Spaniards in 1738, and Andrew, an attorney-at-law, served as advocate for the Reverend George Whitefield when he was summoned to appear before an ecclesiastical court in Charles Town. Andrew married a widow, Sarah Boone Hext, and in 1738, Andrew's step-daughter, fourteen-year-old Sarah Hext, married Dr. John Rutledge. Like her contemporary, Eliza Lucas (who was fifteen in 1738), young Sarah Hext Rutledge was obviously a woman of unusual character and ability.

When Dr. John Rutledge died, Christmas Day, 1750, Sarah was only twenty-six years old with seven young children to rear and educate. She managed a large estate left her by her father, Captain Hugh Hext, including houses in Charles Town, and plantations in Christ Church Parish, Stono, and St. Helena. Ten years separated the births of her oldest son, John, and her youngest child, Edward. Like his older brother John, Edward received his education at Middle Temple in London. He was there at the same time as Thomas Pinckney, younger son of Charles and Eliza Lucas Pinckney. War with England severely interrupted this traditional pattern of study abroad for sons of American colonials.

It is important to note that six of the eleven members of the statehood committee, which reported to the first Provincial Congress of South Carolina, had been Middle Templars—John Rutledge (chairman), Charles Cotesworth Pinckney, Charles Pinckney, Arthur Middleton, Thomas Lynch, Jr., and Thomas Heyward, Jr. The last three, along with Edward Rutledge, were South Carolina's signers of the Declaration of Independence. Edward and his brother attended the first Continental Congress in Philadelphia in 1774. In March, following the adoption of the state constitution, which his committee had proposed, John Rutledge was elected president of the new government in South Carolina and was made commander-in-chief of the army with supreme executive authority. He directed the military activities in South Carolina for the next three years and in 1779 was unanimously chosen governor with dictatorial powers (hence his appellation "Dictator John"). John Rutledge commanded the militia and, at the invasion of South Carolina by the British in 1780, removed to North Carolina where he continued to direct the state's affairs. It was said that *wherever* the carriage of John Rutledge resided, there resided the government of South Carolina.

As "Dictator John" commanded the home front in 1776, his brother, Edward, and Edward's brother-in-law, Arthur Middleton, prepared to join Thomas Lynch, Jr., and Thomas Heyward, Jr., in Philadelphia for that moment in American history that would immortalize their very signatures. The diary of Dr. James Clitherall is a compelling record of his experiences as escort for Mary Izard Middleton and Henrietta Middleton Rutledge as they traveled from Charles Town to Philadelphia in the spring of 1776. Mary and Henrietta were to join their husbands who were delegates to the Continental Congress. The two women and their children were well cared for by Dr. Clitherall whose own words tell it best:

Portrait by Benjamin West.
Photo—R. Alan Powell
Courtesy—Middleton Place Foundation, Charleston, South Carolina.

Arthur (1742–1787) and Mary Izard Middleton (1747–1814) and their son Henry (1770–1846).

Sunday 7th day of April, 1776. I took my leave of Charles Town & proceeded to Goose Creek, where I was disappointed by not meeting Mrs. Arthur Middleton who I expected there to fix on the time & route to the Northern Colonies. Monday—She came up in the morning from Asheley River & I rode over in the afternoon to Mrs. Middleton's. We then determined to set out the next morning; but it being rainy we deferred setting out till

Wednesday 10th. When we departed from Goose Creek, and, as the usual road to Monk's Corner was very bad, we travelled the Strawberry Ferry Road and dined at Monk's Corner, 20 miles. Here we were indifferently entertained upon Bacon and Eggs at Commander's the only public House there. By three o'clock we were on our way to Martin's, a very good House 13 miles further, where we were well entertained by a good obliging brisk Landlord & Lady and received information from Mr. Middleton that the Ferries at Nelson's and Manigault's were on account of ye Freshes impassable. It was therefore necessary to perform a journey of fifty miles the next day

Thursday 11th. We were all up at daylight, the ladies in the carriage at six and we went on to McKelvey's Eutaw 13 miles further....In the Afternoon we proceeded to Col. Thompson's, 23 miles further....

Friday 12th. Col. Thompson (from whose House we had a very beautiful view of the high Hills of Santee) accompanied us through the Lakes, which were formed by the rising of the River...Ferry on the River Congaree is very disagreeable, for the Bushes & Trees were so exceeding thick that the Canoe ran frequently against them & were obliged to be constantly dodging....We left them near five o'clock with Information that the Road to Camden was very good, excepting at one swamp 5 miles further, instead of this, the Badness of the Road benighted us before we got half way, in short it was the worst Road I ever travelled over and it was after nine before we reached Wateree Ferry about 1 1/2 miles from Camden....

Sat. 13th. We received Information That Mr. Middleton, Mr. Heyward and Mr. Burrows had left Camden yesterday Morning, much against Mr. Middleton's Inclination....

Wed. 17th. The first house we called at in No. Carolina was at Robin Crockatt's....At 3 o'clock We were on our Way to Charlotta, sixteen Miles further, but meeting a piece of bad Road & a small Creek the Ladies chose to get out & walk over a Tree that was fallen across. I carried over Henry safely but was not so lucky with Hal for my foot slipping, and the Branch which I held breaking, we fell in the middle of Providence Creek. Hal soon getting dry Clothes the Carriage went on & I dressed myself before about thirty Recruits belonging to the 1st. So. Carolina Rifle Regiment. The Road was so bad that I soon overtook the Carriage & we all proceeded for Charlotta....about half an hour after twilight We were in Town & put up at Patterson's. Immediately after our arrival Lieut. Conyers (who had enlisted the Recruits we met) & Lieut. Armstrong of the 1st Regt. of Provincial Infantry visited us. Lt. Conyers who supped with us gave us a very pleasing description of the flourishing Condition & good Inclination & Affection to the American cause of these People. He said that he supposed there was not two Men in the whole County of Mecklenburgh who was not well affected....& that the People gathered round the Tavern door to gaze with Admiration on Mr. Middleton a day or two before because he was a delegate to the Congress.

Thurs. 18th. In the Morning I went with Lt. Armstrong (who here passed for a Captain & had politely given up his Bed the Night before to Mrs. Rutledge) to pay a visit to his Recruits. They were fine, hearty, well made young Fellows, were very Jolly & sung two spirited songs which I put down not for the Beauty of Expression or turn of Poetry, but to shew their Sentiments. They appear to Disadvantage on Paper but warmed my Heart when sung & accompanied with hearty looks & gestures....

Liberty Song.

You brave Men of Rouen with Pleasure attend
Your Liberty calls you your lives to defend
That Man thats for Liberty let him withdraw
From those that despise their congretional Law.

2

Remember in August in the Year Seventy-five
To raise up a Liberty Pole we did strive
And under Edge Banner declared openly
To stand in defence of our Liberty Tree.

3

Our Land is invaded as plain doth appear
The King he refused Petitions to hear
But let him send over bad Laws to enforce
Boys We with our Musquets will give them a dose.

4

Lord North is the Man who doth publickly say
America's Rich & is able to pay
But that diabolical infernal Foe
Has ruined the King & his Council also.

5

Success to our Captains from each Volunteer
Commissioned with Honor to guard our Frontier
May He that declines from one word that he says
Pull Hemp with Lord North till they both end their days.

6

Success to our Colonel of Charles Town I say
May His commission in Honor still sway
For Love to his Country he always did show
With Armstrong We'll die or We'll conquor our Foe.

7

Success to brave Gadsden the Heathens shall know
That he's our Lieut. and loves us also
And We in return have declared openly
To stand by his side to conquor or die.

8

Success to brave Rollson Boys drink never spare
Invested with Honor our Colors to bear
May he manfully hoist them his Valor to shew
And pull down the Pride of our insolent Foe.

9

Success to our Sergts brave Crawford & Carr
And as for our Corporals We will say thus far
That if they continue so civil & free
They'll gain the good Will of the whole Company.

10

Perhaps you'd be willing or eager to know
Who was the Composer, his station also
He's of no Condition but keeps in the Throng
Boys drink & be merry for he's along.

11

Now to conclude it allmost makes Me mourn
Farewell to the Maids till Home we return
Farewell to our Sweethearts & Comrades also
The drums beat To Arms & away we must go.

Finis

Friday 19th. In the Morning we departed & in a short Mile crossed Rocky River & after passing over twenty-six Miles of pretty good Road arrived at Salisburry. Here the widow Steel kept the best Tavern we had met with Mr. Grimke came in just before dinner from recruiting for the Artillery Regt. and gave Mrs. Middleton a letter from Mr. Middleton informing us that We must take the back Road & he had gone on two days before....

Sat. 20th. ...Mr. Grimké accompanied us over 7 Miles of very bad Roads (which cracked three spokes of one of the hind Carriage Wheels) to the Yadkin Ferry.... We found the broken Wheel so weak as to afford sufficient Ground for uneasiness. Two of the Spokes were clipped whilst we dined on some Ham, Cheese & Biscuit which with the help of Milk & Butter we made an hearty dinner. About 6 O'clock we were on our way for Lindsay's but it growing dark apace We stopped at Bar—Isle's about 3 Miles from our stage & procured a Candle which I held in the Carriage & a Guide. Three Quarters of a Mile had not been travelled over before every spoke in the Wheel cracked & the Carriage was overset so gently indeed that not one of us got hurt, nor even was the Candle put out. We immediately sent off the Coachman to Lindsay's for a Waggon or Cart but were detained in the Cold full two Hours. A Cart at length came & happy were we to get into it. About twelve O'clock we reached the House where they had but two spare Beds in very ordinary small Rooms. The Ladies & Children all lay together in one Bed. The next day

Sun. 21st. Not liking our Situation We sent a Servant on to Guilford Court House with a Letter to Capt. Dent begging he would send an enclosed Letter to Mr. Middleton who we immagined might be somewhere between there & Dick's Ferry & a Stage Wagon to fetch us.... In the Evening the Carriage was brought with a Cart Wheel upon a false Axle Tree & soon After Mr. Middleton surprised us all with his presence. The next Morning

Mon. 22nd. We left Lindsay's for Capt Dent's at Guildford Ct. House & as the Carriage was too weak to carry our Luggage & selves, Mr. & Mrs. Middleton rode in the Chair, Mrs. Rutledge in the Carriage, I on horse back....

Wed. 1st of May. Camp Creek was so high with the Rains that the Ladies were obliged to ride over on horseback....

Saturday 4th. ...after meeting 5 Waggons loaded with Ammunition from Philadelphia for Charlestown arrived at Mc Kintiah's in Leesburg about dusk....

Sunday 12th. Early in the Morning we left Hopkins's & soon met Mr. Rutledge who had received Intelligence of our arrival at Lancaster by Mr. Heyward & Burrows....we spent the rest of the day here in enjoying ourselves & hearing each others supply of News.

Monday 13th. ...we ended our Journey & took Lodgings at Mrs. Yard's, 2nd St., Philadelphia.... In the Metropolis I had an opportunity of seeing the Grand Continental Congress. A body of Men to my knowledge not equaled in History. Men who like Cincinnatus of old have left their Private occupations, taken a temporary leave of their family affairs, disregarded the tender Emotions of Matrimonial, Paternal & Filial Piety & bid adieu to the soft Couch of Luxury to serve three Millions of free People whose Confidence they so much possess that their Advice alone has more weight than the Laws of the most splendid Tyrant decked with all the Trappings of Royalty. O Thou Creator of the Universe Res adspirate Nostras & reward with immortal Honors Men who at the hazard of their Lives have been so forward in asserting the Rights of Mankind & opposing the worst of Tyrants, a King who Syrenlike has covered all his unjust Proceedings with the appearance of Law & Justice thereby deceiving the ignorant Specie Recti.... I soon perceived in this City that Parties ran high. The Body of the People were for Independancy. The Proprietary John Penn & most of the Gentlemen of the City were attached to his Interest were against it lest the form of the Government should be changed & they would no more acknowledge the old Officers of the Government.... A Meeting of the People was called. I attended it. The Paper calling the Meeting was produced recommending a

Number of Resolves. The Committee of Inspection proposed
their Appointment of a Chairman.... About this time the
Great, the Good & Brave Washington arrived to confer with
Congress about the Measures of Campaign 1776. He was admired by the People, revered & respected. His late Generalship
in driving Howe & the British Army from Boston will immortalize his Name & the respect due to one of the Greatest Men
the World ever produced will certainly be paid him by an
American Livy & Verses more sublime than Homers.... I forgot to mention that before the meeting of the Conference every
method was taken to force Men into Independancy by this
Body. They put the Question to the City Batallions *under Arms*
& any Man who dared oppose their opinion was insulted &
hushed by their Interruptions, sneers, & hissings.... I was as
happy here as the abscence of my relations would permit. After living 1 month at Mrs. Yard's Mr. Middleton & Rutledge
invited me to live with them & here I experienced much Happiness in the pleasure of Mrs. Middleton's conversation. A Lady
who is one of the first of her sex for sense, politeness & every
female accomplishment. Mrs. Rutledge was generally sick &
the G. at Congress.

July 2nd. This glorious day that threw off the Tyranny of George
3rd. and greeted these Colonies as free united & independant
States I left Philadelphia having heard yesterday that an attack
on New York was expected hourly....

Presumably Mary Middleton and Henrietta Rutledge had many further adventures to tell their friend and relative Harriott when they returned to stay with her at Hampton.

Chapter 5

Political activity in Philadelphia in July 1776 was preceded to the south by a day-and-night military effort to fortify Charles Town from attack by the British. Christopher Gadsden had been successful in convincing the Continental Congress to establish a Continental navy, which his fellow delegate, Edward Rutledge, had likened to an infant seizing a mad bull by the horns. Gadsden's proposal had a similar effect on South Carolina's Provincial Congress. John Rutledge offered to ride without stopping to Philadelphia to assist in reuniting Great Britain and America.

In the end the two Rutledge brothers and other conservative forces, hoping for reconciliation rather than war, were convinced of the necessity for absolute independence. This did not come by Christopher Gadsden's appeal for naval force nor by circulation of Thomas Paine's inciteful pamphlet *Common Sense,* but rather by the reported appearance of British warships and troop transports preparing for rendezvous off the North Carolina coast. On June 28, 1776, the British fleet (fifty-two ships strong) opened fire on the palmetto-log fortification at Sullivan's Island, offshore from Charles Town. Colonel Christopher Gadsden commanded his troops of the First Provincial Regiment, led by Lieutenant Colonel Charles Cotesworth Pinckney and Captain Thomas Pinckney, to strengthen southern shore defenses across the harbor at Fort Johnson. Colonel William Moultrie and the fifteen hundred men of his Second Provincial Regiment had labored to finish the fort on the north side of Sullivan's Island. Thomas Pinckney had written his sister, Harriott, that her husband, Colonel Daniel Horry, was on Sullivan's Island and was "among the Number with 300 of his Regiment."

Colonel Horry's assignment was to support the advance post of Colonel William Thompson's Rangers. They were to prevent Sir Henry Clinton and Major General Lord Cornwallis from crossing the inlet to Sullivan's Island with the three-thousand-strong British force of regulars and marines. The patriots were successful on land, as was Moultrie, who with his regiment defended the log fort with 4,766 pounds of powder against the British use of 34,000 pounds. The British warships withdrew, bringing an end to anxiety in Charles Town over silence from the island. It was feared that Moultrie had surrendered when indeed careful, deliberate use of 500 pounds of gunpowder, sent by President John Rutledge late that afternoon, had, for the time being, driven back the British fleet. The Royal navy had intended an easy take-over to the south in order to weaken New England resistance. The South Carolina patriots had turned back the forces sent against them and had defended the southern colonies against occupation. The following September, the palmetto-log fort on Sullivan's Island was renamed Fort Moultrie to honor William Moultrie.

This victory, along with news that the South Carolina delegation in Philadelphia had turned the tide by voting in favor of Richard Henry Lee's resolution declaring independence, caused great celebration in Charles Town. Coincidentally Charles Town received word of the Declaration on August 2, the day the South Carolina delegates actually signed Thomas Jefferson's carefully worded document. There was a grand procession in Charles Town on August 5, 1776, led by President John Rutledge, who was accompanied by Charles Cotesworth and Thomas Pinckney. All civil and military officers participated in the parade and ceremonies at the Liberty Tree, a live oak located just outside the city.

The Declaration of Independence was read to those assembled by Major Barnard Elliott, and an address was delivered by the Reverend William Percy, a young minister of strong patriot sentiments who frequently occupied the pulpit of St. Michael's Church. Although South Carolinians had been hesitant to break their ties with England, the recent attack on their harbor by the British navy swayed public opinion toward absolute independence and caused favorable reception of the action taken by their delegation to the Continental Congress in Philadelphia that eventful July.

Chapter 6

On September 20, 1776, the Pinckney brothers became officers in the regular army (First South Carolina Regiment, Continental Line) established by the Continental Congress. Their supreme commander was George Washington. The ensuing months saw no peace, and the families staying at Hampton Plantation were eager to learn of the developing war with the British forces. Thomas Pinckney was especially attentive to his mother and sister in writing detailed accounts of his actions and any news of Charles Cotesworth and Daniel Horry.

In June 1777 the young Marquis de Lafayette and Johann Kalb (Baron de Kalb), accompanied by eleven French officers, arrived in Charles Town. They were met and entertained by the Pinckneys, who conversed fluently in French about their experiences in France when they were in school at the Royal Military Academy in Caen. Within a few weeks Charles Cotesworth and Daniel Horry were given the opportunity to join Lafayette twenty miles north of Philadelphia at General Washington's headquarters. Lafayette, a nineteen-year-old French nobleman, had offered to join the patriots' cause without pay.

Pinckney and Horry were received by Washington on August 19, 1777, and served on the General's staff until the following year when Pinckney returned to join his brother in an expedition against St. Augustine in the Florida territory. This effort failed due to the advance of the British general Augustine Prevost. The patriots were pushed back to Charles Town with Thomas helping to stem this tide at the Stono River. Both brothers took part in the defense of Savannah, Georgia, with Thomas now serving as a major. Horry returned to South Carolina in 1779 to raise a regiment of dragoons. This assignment was well suited to Horry's expertise as a horseman and developed into a full command for Horry of General Moultrie's forces in the area near Dorchester.

In May 1779 General Prevost ordered destruction of the plantation homes on his path to Charles Town. Among the first to be burned was Auckland, the Pinckney home on the Ashepoo River, which had been the family's choice as the safest location for valuables and all the archival material and books of Chief Justice Charles Pinckney, which had been left to Thomas. Prevost's troops also destroyed all but the brick frame of Eliza Pinckney's plantation home, Belmont.

Harriott Pinckney Horry, aware of Prevost's destructive march, had moved her mother from Belmont to Hampton Plantation where they were joined by Sally Pinckney, Henrietta Rutledge, Hester Drayton, Mary Izard Middleton, and Lady Mary Middleton. There were six other prominent women housed there, plus the grandchildren of Eliza Pinckney, bringing the population of Hampton to its capacity.

On hearing of the destruction of the Pinckney homes by the British, Eliza Lucas Pinckney wrote her son Thomas from Hampton:

> My Dear Tomm—I have just received your letter with the account of my losses, and your almost ruined fortunes by the enemy. A severe blow! but I feel not for myself, but for you; 'tis for your losses my greatly beloved child that I grieve; the loss of fortune could affect me little, but that it will deprive my dear Children of my assistance when they may stand most in need of it. One happiness I have ever enjoyed,—that of being free from avarice, which will lighten the present evil with regard to myself; and a very little, at my time of life will be sufficient.... Your Brother's [Charles Cotesworth Pinckney's] truly generous offer to divide what remains to him among us, is worthy of him. I am greatly affected but not surprised at his liberality.
>
> I know his disinterdness, his sensibility and affection. You say, I must be sensible you can't agree to this offer; indeed my dear Tomm I

Photo—R. Alan Powell
Courtesy—Second Regiment, South Carolina Line.

Continental Army reenactment at Middleton Place (1976) with tents recognizable as being under the Middleton Oaks.

am very sensible of it, nor can I take a penny from his young helpless family. Independence is all I want and a little will make us that. Don't grieve for me my child as I assure you I do not for myself. While I have such children dare I think my lot hard? God forbid! I pray the Almighty disposes of events to preserve them and my grandchildren to me, and for all the rest I hope I shall be able to say not only contentedly but cheerfully, God's sacred will be done!

When British generals Clinton and Arbuthnot approached Charles Town, Charles Cotesworth was given command of Fort Moultrie due to the resignation of Brigadier General Christopher Gadsden. The Pinckney brothers argued against surrender and so with the fall of Charles Town, in 1780, Charles Cotesworth was taken prisoner. Thomas escaped by taking a mission for General Benjamin Lincoln and was attached to a unit commanded by Horatio Gates on the high road to the south. His leg was shattered at Camden, South Carolina, in a battle which took the life of Lafayette's friend, Baron de Kalb. He was an invalid prisoner at the Motte home, Mount Joseph (renamed Fort Motte), where he was cared for by his wife and her family. On July 12, 1779, he had married Elizabeth [Betsey] Motte, daughter of Rebecca Brewton and Jacob Motte, Jr. The Mottes had no objections to a wartime marriage for their daughter. Betsey's grandparents, the senior Jacob Mottes, had been longtime friends of Eliza and Charles Pinckney, and it was at their home, Mount Pleasant, that Charles Pinckney had stayed in an effort to recover from the fever that took his life in 1758.

Thomas Pinckney was returned to Charles Town as soon as his injury would permit, and by 1781 the entire family was in the hands of the British. In 1780 Mrs. Motte and her three daughters were "detained" in the Charles Town home she inherited from her brother, Miles Brewton. First Sir Henry Clinton and then Lord Rawdon, British officers, occupied her home, whereupon she kept her daughters locked in the attic, for fear the rumors about mistreatment of townspeople by their captors might prove to be true.

Gabriel Manigault kept a diary from 1774 to 1784 in which he recorded the occupation of Charles Town by the British. Gabriel's grandfather, Peter Manigault, had served as speaker of the South Carolina Common's House of Assembly from 1765 to 1772 and was an outspoken advocate for resistance to the Stamp Act and other Royal controls. Gabriel's father, Gabriel, Sr., designed several buildings in Charles Town including the Joseph Manigault home on Meeting Street. The younger Gabriel wrote clearly of those events in May 1780:

Photo—R. Alan Powell
Courtesy—Second Regiment, South Carolina Line.

Marching drummers of the Continental Army reenactment during the United States bicentennial (1976).

8th May. Early in the morning the British sent in a flag, which brought on a truce that continued 2 days and 1 night. This gave an expectation of the seige being concluded.

9th. Hostilities began again at $9^1/2$ o'Clock in the evening. The fire now kept up on both sides was really dreadful, and within our lines did great execution.

10th. It being supposed by the inhabitants and Citizens of Charlestown that General Lincoln had refused to accept the terms offered yesterday by the enemy, on account of some articles which related to them; 500 of them presented to him a petition this afternoon, declaring their approbation of the terms offered, and praying that he would agree to them.

11th. In consequence of the above petition a Flag was sent to the British about 2 o'Clock, P.M. to treat about a Capitulation.

12 May. At about 9 o'Clock A.M. Charlestown capitulated. At 2 o'Clock, P.M. the American Army marched out of, and the British Army marched into, Charlestown.

Colonel Daniel Horry, active against the British from the very beginning, made an unfortunate choice following the fall of Charles Town. He had successfully escaped an ambush by Lieutenant Colonel Banastre Tarleton by hiding in the swamp. When the enemy entered the area of the Santee, Horry "took protection," that is, deserted the patriot cause, for fear that his property and indeed his family would be subjected to harm or complete destruction. A letter June 11, 1780, from Thomas Pinckney to Harriott told of his unhappiness at his brother-in-law's decision:

I need not say that if I thought I could remain at home consistently with my principles I should not think of proceeding but let my path be what it may, I hope I shall not act in such a way as to call up a blush on the Cheek of those who wish me well. The trial is at present rather severe but I firmly trust that we shall not be entirely given up to misfortune. Certain I am that matters are not so bad with us as the despondency of our own People and the high hopes of our adversaries would induce you to think.

Tho' I am very sorry for the step Col. Horry has taken in one sense, yet it can not but give me the greatest pleasure to consider that you will have a Person with you to support & protect you. Adieu, my Dearest Friend & may Heaven protect & make you Bear this cloud with Resignation.

Wartime continued to make life difficult for many people connected with Hampton. By January 1781 Thomas Pinckney, his wife Betsey, and their infant son, Tom, were allowed to move to Charles Town because Thomas' leg needed surgical care. They occupied the town house belonging to Daniel and Harriott at 66 Broad Street. The Horrys and Eliza Pinckney were at Hampton during this period, and Charles Cotesworth was a prisoner at Snee Farm, the estate of his cousin, Charles Pinckney II, five miles from Haddrell's Point. In August 1780 Arthur Middleton was taken, on the prison ship *Jersey,* to St. Augustine, Florida, where he and fifty-one other prominent Charlestonians were held captive one year. Also Edward Rutledge and Thomas Heyward, Jr., were exiled in St. Augustine—all three surviving South Carolina signers of the Declaration of Independence were there (Thomas Lynch, Jr., had died at sea in

Photo—R. Alan Powell
Courtesy—Second Regiment, South Carolina Line.

Continental Army battle reenactment with Middleton Place House in the background (1976).

1779). In July 1781 they were exchanged for British officers who were American prisioners of war. The place of exchange was Philadelphia, and all families of the St. Augustine prisoners were ordered out of South Carolina by August 1. Charles Cotesworth, Thomas, their wives and children, the families of Edward Rutledge and many others were affected. The Pinckney and Rutledge families were housed in the brick mansion, Stenton, in Germantown which was about ten miles outside Philadelphia. The home had been the headquarters of General Washington in August 1777 and then later occupied by Sir William Howe, the general in command of British forces at the Battle of Germantown.

Stenton, at best, was uncomfortable and shabby by this time. The period of use by commanding military personnel of both armies had caused this once fine home of Philadelphia surgeon Dr. George Logan to bear evidence of its neglect. Ten persons from three families utilized the available space to the best of their capabilities: Charles Cotesworth and Sally Pinckney, their daughters—Maria Henrietta and Harriott; Thomas and Betsey Pinckney, their son—Thomas, Jr.; and Edward and Henrietta Rutledge, their son—Henry Middleton Rutledge. It was not an easy time for any of them and as Charles Cotesworth wrote his mother on July 25, "Continental money does not pass here."

Chapter 7

Governor John Rutledge reconvened the General Assembly of South Carolina at the village of Jacksonborough on January 18, 1782. The 1778 South Carolina Constitution had decreed that the General Assembly would meet the first Monday in January, and the meeting—though delayed—was a brave gesture in view of the fact that the British were only thirty-five miles away in Charles Town. General Nathanael Greene stationed his army nearby to protect the representatives.

An immediate aim of the Assembly was to confiscate property of Tories and to amerce, or tax, former patriots who had taken British protection. This action was part vengeance and part desperation, to procure funds for the South Carolina military. Among those who had been elected in 1781 to be a part of this Assembly were Thomas Pinckney and Charles Cotesworth. However, the prisoner exchange did not occur in time for them to attend the Assembly, which adjourned February 26.

Edward Rutledge, who was exchanged earlier, left his family with the Pinckneys at Stenton, in Pennsylvania, and attended the Assembly convened by his brother, "Dictator John." Edward tried to keep close friends and family from suffering severe losses, yet he favored amercement in general. As privy councilor, he was able to minimize infliction of heavy punishment, which some administered to vent their private resentments, but he was unable to prevent the levying of penalties altogether. Concerning the twelve percent amercement given Colonel Daniel Horry, Edward Rutledge wrote: "Horry had many friends, but they were unsuccessfull. Indeed, had it not been for the many Virtues of the Pinckneys, his Estate would unquestionably have been confiscated."

In August 1781, Daniel Horry had taken his son, twelve-year-old Daniel, Jr., to London to enroll him in Westminster School. Delegates to the General Assembly could not forgive Horry for his desertion during a time when they felt he could have helped secure the area around the Santee River. The patriots had suffered much loss and hardship during the months of occupation by the British, and it was decided that those who were given penalties must come out from "protection" in British-held Charles Town by the next scheduled meeting of the Assembly (August 1782) or have their estates confiscated and be banished from the state.

JOHN RUTLEDGE.

John Rutledge (1739–1800).

Arthur Middleton, still attending sessions of the Continental Congress in Philadelphia, was kept informed as to the activities of those amerced men by frequent correspondence with his brothers-in-law, Charles Cotesworth Pinckney and Edward Rutledge. "Ned" Rutledge who had successfully kept his elderly father-in-law, Henry Middleton, from being listed for amercement, wrote Arthur in Philadelphia that he wished he were there and told him, "passions of some People run very high ... it is an odious painful Business."

Charles Cotesworth Pinckney used as much persuasion as possible to convince those "protection men" closest to him that escaping penalty would bring further embarrassment to their families and to themselves. His first cousin, Charles Pinckney II (owner of Snee Farm), also had received a twelve percent amercement on his property. Charles Cotesworth wrote him, offering to put up security to prevent the sale of his property. This letter finally persuaded Cousin Charles to leave British protection. On August 13, 1782, Charles Cotesworth wrote to Arthur Middleton with the following news: "My Cousin is at length come out of Town and also a prodigious number of refugees...."

Charles Cotesworth's brother-in-law, Daniel Horry, returned to Charles Town by ship from London and then was detained by the very forces who were supposed to shield him. He made application to leave town but was repeatedly refused. On March 16, 1782, Edward Rutledge wrote Arthur Middleton: "Poor Horry...I have sent my Opinion as to his Line of Conduct—It is really a cruel Case. They can give no kind of Protection to his Property, & yet they detain his Person."

Harriott Horry wrote letters, from Hampton Plantation, pleading her husband's case. Her aid to the ragged troops commanded by General Francis Marion (the Swamp Fox) had become legendary along the Santee.

Harriott Horry Rutledge Ravenel wrote in 1906 concerning her great-grandmother, Harriott Pinckney Horry:

> Tarleton sometimes played the fine gentleman on these raids; as when at Mrs. Horry's at Hampton, South Santee (where the fidelity of the servants and the coolness of the mistress alone saved Marion from falling into his hands), he took for his share of the spoil only a fine copy of Milton; his men were less forbearing. Other commanders (Major Fraser for instance) were more frankly brutal. Mrs. Horry tells how he took her watch and a miniature of her friend Mrs. Blake of Newington, which she wore at her neck.

Harriott Horry had reason to defend her property against any unjust penalty. In her arguments she noted that her mother and brothers, though remaining loyal, had lost their estates to the British and could not come to Horry's aid. The once wealthy Pinckney family, indeed the entire state of South Carolina, was bankrupt. This fact only encouraged harsh judgment on those who had acknowledged British authority. Daniel Horry would be no exception. It must have seemed a desperate, hopeless situation to Eliza and Harriott. With no help from either side, they had only sacrifice, hardship, and disappointment to look forward to. Charles Pinckney II, weakened by humiliation and despair, contracted "country fever" soon after leaving Charles Town. He died on September 22, 1782, and Charles Cotesworth wrote to his sister, Harriott, that his cousin "was a man of worth."

It is of importance to note that the British Parliament voted in late May 1782 to end efforts to control the American Colonies by force, to end hostilities, and to establish peace. In spite of this move, Charles Town was not liberated until December 14, 1782. Seven months of anxiety only prolonged the hardships already endured. Delays were caused by difficulties in securing safe passage for over nine thousand Loyalists as well as a multitude of Negro slaves being carried away as plunder. During the war an estimated twenty-five thousand slaves were taken from South Carolina alone. They were not to be freed, but were transported to the West Indies and sold. Three hundred British ships were used to strip Charles Town, while ten armed engagements took place in South Carolina following the surrender of Cornwallis in Virginia. The city was tightly held, and many feared that the final act of evacuation would be the burning of what was left. For this reason, General Nathanael Greene negotiated an agreement allowing Continental forces to enter the city as the British withdrew. At daybreak liberation began. The American troops followed some two hundred yards behind the departing British armies. The joyful day was recorded by Gabriel Manigault:

> 14th Decr. 1782. This day the British Army evacuated Charlestown, and a few days after I went there, after an absence of about a year, during which time I had been generally obliged to take up my abode in some friends house, it having been unsafe, on account of the british Troops to remain at any plantation of my own.

A general peace was not declared until mid-April 1783; the last troops left South Carolina by transport in July; a definitive treaty of peace was signed in London on September 3; and on November 3, 1783, Charles Cotesworth Pinckney was commissioned brigadier general by brevet, and the American army was ordered disbanded by commander-in-chief, General George Washington.

Chapter 8

The year 1783 saw the end of hostilities with Britain, the disbanding of the army, and the beginning of "these United States." The country was free but far from united. The thirteen former colonies jealously guarded their individual rights, were suspicious of centralized controls, and were generally slow to conform to the Articles of Confederation established by Congress in 1777. However, as several foreign nations recognized the independence of the new nation, a sense of national unity began to take hold.

In South Carolina, Charles Town declared herself a city not a town, and the name was changed to Charleston. Those military leaders from throughout the state who had struggled valiantly for America's independence while Charles Town was held captive, now demanded that low-country city no longer dominate South Carolina government. Following much bitter dispute, the center of the state was chosen, and the new city of Columbia was established as a more accessible capital. The legislature met there for the first time in 1790.

Following the war, life at Hampton Plantation was busy and productive. Daniel Horry, thought by some to be broken in spirit due to his decision to accept protection from the British, quietly withdrew from active public life. He was still respected by many of his neighbor planters and, in July 1785, represented St. James Santee at the Second Convention of the Protestant Episcopal Church in South Carolina. It was obvious that his concerns centered around his church affiliations and his goals for the restoration of Hampton as an agricultural leader among the Santee plantations. The cultivation of tide-water rice became extremely vital to Horry and to other low-country planters.

Harriott Horry's mother, Eliza Pinckney, maintained her residence at Hampton. Her home plantation, Belmont, was no longer productive. All that had remained of the grand showplace in 1783 had been the house which was burned accidentally that year by slaves who were there to cut wood. The Pinckney brothers, who resumed their law practices, also busied themselves with cultivation and the restoration of their town houses and plantations. Charles Cotesworth and his brother-in-law, Edward Rutledge, became involved in assisting their fellow citizens in the collection of debts and in the untangling of property matters. They

41

were both listed as prosperous, by 1796, with earnings of 3,500 to 4,500 pounds sterling a year. It was a serious task to rebuild family fortunes, and their efforts were complicated by sorrow.

In 1784, Sally Middleton Pinckney died following a long battle with tuberculosis. This left thirty-eight-year-old Charles Cotesworth Pinckney a widower with three daughters under ten years of age (two sons, each named Charles Cotesworth, Jr., died as infants in 1779/1780). He placed Maria Henrietta, Harriott, and Eliza Lucas with their Grandmother Pinckney and the Horry family at Hampton. Charles Cotesworth then immersed himself in his work and political duties. He was confident of the many advantages his daughters would receive at the Santee plantation.

In November of the following year Daniel Horry died at Hampton. He suffered liver failure and bilious fever, which caused an agonizing death. With the passing of Hampton's owner, Harriott Pinckney Horry became responsible for the plantation's management. Daniel Horry's will gave Harriott use of Hampton for her lifetime with ownership going to their sixteen-year-old son Daniel, Jr., who had remained in Europe for his education, had become Francophile, and eventually was married to Elenore Marie Florimonde de Fay La Tour Marbourg, niece of the Marquis de Lafayette. The young Horry also changed his name to Charles Lucas Pinckney Horry and maintained very little interest in South Carolina or his native Hampton. His sister, Harriott, was fifteen at the time of their father's death and was by no means lonely since the arrival of her three cousins, Charles Cotesworth's daughters.

Hampton flourished as a rice plantation under the able management of Mrs. Horry and her mother, and they shared commercial shipping costs with Thomas Pinckney, who had given up his law practice, had purchased Fairfield and Eldorado plantations on the Santee, and was restoring his inheritance, Auckland Plantation.

Harriott Horry's boat, *Shipwell,* was large enough to be used for transporting goods both from Hampton and other nearby Santee plantations to Charleston. In 1786 she purchased an elegant English coach, made to her specifications. Her income was profitable enough for the addition, sometime before 1790, of the handsome Adamesque portico that graces the front of Hampton. It was the earliest portico of this style in the south and may well reveal the Pinckney influence on the home. When Harriott was a young girl she and her parents, Charles and Eliza Pinckney, spent several years in England staying near a great house named Hampton, on the Thames River. The owner of *that* Hampton was

Photo—R. Alan Powell
Courtesy—Benjamin Bosworth Smith, Charleston, South Carolina.

Handpainted silk dress that belonged to Harriott Pinckney Horry (1748–1830)—worn by her great-great-granddaughter, Mary Middleton Rutledge Reese Smith.

the famous English actor, David Garrick. During the Pinckney stay on the Thames (1752-1758), Garrick commissioned a portico to be designed by the Adams brothers for his villa. This addition evidently caused much favorable comment among his guests, and it is reasonable to assume that Eliza Pinckney persuaded Harriott to add a similar portico to their large home on the Santee. Whatever the origin of its name (first documented in 1769) or its portico (c. 1790), Hampton's reticent beauty delighted visitors whether their approach was from Wambaw Creek or the drive from the King's Highway.

Chapter 9

By 1790, the ravages of war behind them, the citizens of South Carolina were slowly regaining their former dignity and manner of living. Plantations and town houses alike were refurbished; flower gardens, in greater variety and abundance than ever before, adorned Charleston's piazza-styled yard openings; and a renewed prosperity and optimism filled the air.

By early spring of 1791, news of the proposed southern tour of the country's first president, George Washington, had consumed the industrious people of Charleston with plans for his arrival and stay in their fair city. The extremely popular Washington had been elected in 1789 by an admiring citizenry. Banners and bandeaux inscribed with mottoes were designed months in advance of his visit. White hair-ribbons, painted with the president's likeness and encircled by the words "God bless our President," were made and distributed to the ladies, along with sashes inscribed with the legend "Hail to the Father of our Country." Breakfasts, balls, and banquets were planned, the invitations to which were treasured for generations to come. Readied for its illustrious guest, the home of Thomas Heyward, Jr., was furnished and prepared with the single object in mind of providing every possible comfort and accommodation. Everywhere the grateful patriots could not seem to do enough for this man whom they praised as "the Great, the Good and Brave Washington." By the end of April the rivers and roads along his itinerary had become virtual red carpets of welcome for this most honored guest, and the first of May found all of Charleston breathlessly awaiting his arrival.

The approach to Charleston from Wilmington along the King's Highway was a continuation of sand and pine for Washington, with one exception. The richly cultivated rice fields were of extreme interest to him as he was an agricultural enthusiast and planter himself.

Because there were few stands (inns) for travelers, private homes along the way were ceremoniously opened to the president. One such stop recorded in his diary was Hampton. Harriott Horry, with her mother, Eliza Lucas Pinckney, provided a late breakfast and dinner for the entire retinue en route to Charleston. For generations to come it was told that Washington recommended to Mrs. Horry that she spare the live oak tree in front of the portico which she thought would grow to detract from the portico's beauty and obstruct the view. The tree was not removed and bears the name, "Washington Oak." A chariot was designed by David Clark of Philadelphia especially for Washington's journey. Four horses pulled it, with the president's favorite horse led behind for his convenience at crossings. Several outriders accompanied the president, and prominent gentlemen from Charleston rode out a day or two in advance to welcome and escort him to their city. In his diary Washington recorded his own impressions of post-Revolution Charleston and his reception there:

MAY

Sunday, first. Left Georgetown about 6 o'clock and crossing the Santee Creek at the Town, and the Santee River 12 miles from it, at Lynch's Island, we breakfasted and dined at Mrs. Horry's [Hampton Plantation] about 15 miles from Georgetown and lodged at the Plantation of Mr. Manigold [sic; Gabriel Manigault] about 19 miles farther.

Monday, 2d. Breakfasted at the Country seat of Govr. Pinckney [Charles, III; thirty-one-year-old great nephew of Chief Justice Charles Pinckney and immediate successor to Governor Thomas Pinckney] about 18 miles from our lodging place, and then came to the ferry at Haddrel's point, 6 miles further, where I was met by the Recorder of the City [John Bee Holmes], General Pinckney [Charles Cotesworth] and Edward Rutledge [brother of "Dictator John"], Esqr, in a 12 oared barge rowed by 12 American Captains of Ships, most elegantly dressed. There were a great number of other Boats with Gentlemen and ladies in them; and two Boats with Music; all of whom attended me across, and on the passage were met by a number of others. As we approached the town a salute with artillery commenced, and at the Wharf I was met by the Governor [Charles Pinckney III], the Lt. Governor [Isaac Holmes], the Intendt. of the City [Arnoldus Vanderhorst]; the two Senators of the State [Pierce Butler and Ralph Izard], Wardens of the City; Cincinnati, etc. etc. and conducted to the Exchange where they passed by in procession; from thence I was conducted in like manner to my lodgings; after which I dined at the Governors (in what he called a private way) with 15 or 18 Gentlemen....

The lodgings provided for me in this place were very good, being the furnished house of a Gentleman [Thomas Heyward, Jr.] at present in the Country; but occupied by a person placed there on purpose to accomodate [sic] me, and who was paid in the same manner as any other letter of lodgings would have been paid [Mrs. Rebecca Jamieson].

Courtesy—Middleton Place Foundation, Charleston, South Carolina.

Portrait of George Washington by William R. Birch (1755–1834) in 1797. In front (left to right) are an early medal of the Society of the Cincinnati, a gold shoe buckle that belonged to Arthur Middleton, and a gold patch box that belonged to his wife, Mary.

Tuesday, 3d. Breakfasted with Mrs. Rutledge [Elizabeth Grimké Rutledge] (the Lady of the Chief Justice of the State [John Rutledge; first governor of South Carolina] who was on the Circuits) and dined with the Citizens at a public dinr. given by them at the Exchange.

Was visited about 2 O'clock, by a great number of the most respectable ladies of Charleston—the first honor of the kind I had ever experienced and it was as flattering as it was singular.

Wednesday, 4th. Dined with the Members of the Cincinnati [from the Society's preamble (1783): "the Officers of the American Army do hereby constitute themselves a Society of Friends; and possessing the highest veneration for the character of that illustrious Roman, Lucius Quinctius Cincinnatus, denominate themselves 'THE SOCIETY OF THE CINCINNATI.' "] and in the evening went to a very elegant dancing Assembly at the Exchange, at which were 256 elegantly dressed and handsome ladies.

In the forenoon (indeed before breakfast to day) I visited and examined the lines of attack and defence of the City....

Thursday, 5th. Visited the works of Fort Johnson James' Island, and Fort Moultree [sic] on Sullivan's Island; both of which are in Ruins, and scarcely a trace of the latter left, the former quite fallen.

Dined with a very large Company at the Governor's, and in the evening went to a Concert at the Exchange at wch. there were at least 400 ladies the number and appearance of wch. exceeded any thing of the kind I had ever seen.

Friday, 6th. Viewed the town on horseback by riding through most of the principal Streets.

Dined at Majr. Butler's [Pierce Butler] and went to a Ball in the evening at the Governors where there was a select Company of ladies.

Saturday, 7th. Before Break[fast] I visited the Orphan House at which there were one hundred and seven boys and girls. This appears to be a charitable institution and under good management. I also viewed the City from the balcony of [Saint Michael's] Church from whence the whole is seen in one view and to advantage, the Gardens and green trees which are interspersed adding much to the beauty of the prospect.

Charleston stands on a Pininsula [sic] between the Ashley and Cooper Rivers and contains about 1600 dwelling houses and nearly 16,000 Souls of which about 8000 are white. It lies low with unpaved streets (except the footways) of sand. There are a number of very good houses of Brick and wood but most of the latter. The Inhabitants are wealthy, Gay, and Hospitable; appear happy and satisfied with the Genl. Government. A cut is much talked of between the Ashley and Santee Rivers but it would seem I think, as if the accomplishment of the measure was not very near. It would be a great thing for Charleston if it could be effected. The principal exports from this place is [sic] Rice, Indigo, and Tobacco; of the last from 5 to 8000 Hhds. have been exported, and of the first from 80 to 120,000 Barrels.

Sunday, 8th. Went to Crowded Churches in the morning and afternoon. To [Saint Philip's] in the morning and [Saint Michael's] in the afternoon.

Dined with General Moultree [sic].

Monday, 9th. At six o'clock I recommenced my journey for Savanna [sic]; attended by a Corps of the Cincinnati and most of the principal Gentlemen of the City as far as the bridge over Ashley River....

Of his tour Washington commented later that he especially remembered the women of Charleston. His brief visit with Eliza Lucas Pinckney at Hampton Plantation during his triumphant southern tour must have been a memorable time for him. He respected her accomplishments, and had not forgotten the service her sons had rendered the American colonies during the war with Britain. His presidential administration was distinguished by the multitude of high-level positions he offered both Thomas and Charles Cotesworth Pinckney as well as John and Edward Rutledge. The Pinckney/Rutledge integrity and loyalty had gone unquestioned through the years of the Revolution, and George Washington entreated these extraordinary men from South Carolina to remain closely tied to him and to the government of their young nation. The president offered cabinet posts, judgeships, and foreign diplomatic missions to these most trusted fellow members of the Society of the Cincinnati.

In 1791 Thomas Pinckney, lately governor of South Carolina [1787–1789] accepted an appointment from Washington as minister to London. He moved there with his family and undertook the heavy responsibility of helping to maintain peace with Britain. At the same time, he was to secure American commericial rights as well as compensation for the twenty-five thousand slaves that had been forcibly removed in 1782 by the British army. From there, Thomas Pinckney was appointed to a special mission to Spain and his brother, Charles Cotesworth, was sent as ambassador to France. During the 1790s Washington depended greatly on the diplomatic skills of these two brothers to keep American negotiations strong yet peaceful.

Thomas Jefferson was secretary of state when Thomas Pinckney, his wife Betsey, their five children, and Edward Rutledge's daughter Sarah finally sailed for London in June 1792. The letters of instruction from Jefferson to Thomas Pinckney began with the following introduction:

> I have already had the honor of delivering to you your commission as Minister Plenipotentiary of the United States at the Court of London, and now that of enclosing your letter of credence to the King [George III], sealed, and a copy of it open for your information....

His was a difficult mission, yet one to which the well-spoken, European-educated Pinckney was ideally suited.

Personal sorrow added weight to his awesome responsibilities. Thomas had known that his mother was not well when he left for London, but he had been comforted by the news that she had gone to Philadelphia for specialized treatment of the breast cancer that threatened her life. George Washington had secured for Eliza the services of his own physician, Dr. James Tate, who was, in the president's own words to Thomas, "possessed of the valuable secret of curing Cancerous complaints." Tate's non-surgical techniques were far advanced for that day, not generally accepted by medical circles outside Philadelphia, and, unfortunately, proved unsuccessful in this particular case.

So it was that Thomas and his family as well as Charles Cotesworth and his second wife, Mary Stead [wealthy granddaughter of Robert Johnson, South Carolina Royal governor, 1730–1735], received the shocking news that the Pinckney matriarch, the only parent her three children had ever known, had suffered greatly from May 10 until her death on May 26. Eliza Pinckney had been accompanied to Philadelphia by her daughter, Harriott, and by the granddaughters she had helped to rear at Hampton. Now it was their sad task to arrange for Eliza's funeral and to return home without her.

Eliza Lucas Pinckney was buried in St. Peter's Episcopal churchyard in Philadelphia, May 27, 1793. Her friend and her president, George Washington, requested the honor of serving as pall bearer. His own grief, as well as his long-standing gratitude to the entire family, could have found no better expression. Eliza's sons were truly sons of America, absent from their mother's final rites only because of the distance involved in continued service to their country. This was Washington's compassionate effort to, in some way, be of service to them.

In little more than a year, Thomas Pinckney's "adorable Miss Betsey" was dead at age thirty-two. Her unexpected death in London, August 24, 1794, was an immense shock to Thomas and to his family in South Carolina. For the Pinckneys and the Horrys, the decade of restoration that followed the final British evacuation of Charleston and been productive, though marked by sadness. The loss of Charles Cotesworth's wife, Sally Middleton Pinckney, in 1784, Daniel Horry in 1785, and Eliza Lucas Pinckney in 1793 had drastically changed life at Hampton, while deaths within the Middleton and Rutledge families only had added to their grief: Henry Middleton in 1784; Arthur Middleton in 1787; Lady Mary Middleton in 1788; and Henrietta Middleton Rutledge [wife of Edward] and Sarah Hext Rutledge [widow of Dr. John] the same day in 1792, followed in six months by the death of Elizabeth Grimké Rutledge [wife of "Dictator John"].

Throughout this period, Harriott, Thomas, and Charles Cotesworth maintained the same remarkable courage that had been demonstrated for them by their mother. Life for Eliza Lucas Pinckney had been filled with purpose and dedication, with little time spent nurturing her own aloneness and personal griefs. Her sons distinguished themselves in public life; her daughter was a successful planter, an accomplished household manager, and a refined, gracious hostess of the most magnificent home on the Santee—Hampton Plantation.

Part III

THE SPINSTER

Harriott Pinckney Horry [Rutledge] (1770–1858)

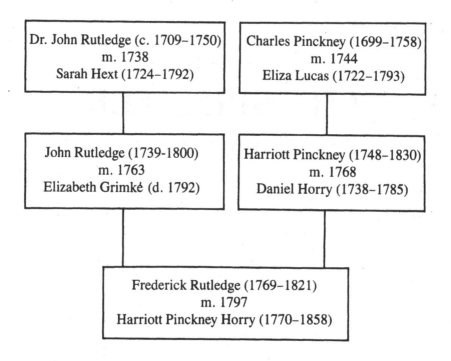

Dr. John Rutledge (c. 1709–1750)
m. 1738
Sarah Hext (1724–1792)

Charles Pinckney (1699–1758)
m. 1744
Eliza Lucas (1722–1793)

John Rutledge (1739-1800)
m. 1763
Elizabeth Grimké (d. 1792)

Harriott Pinckney (1748–1830)
m. 1768
Daniel Horry (1738–1785)

Frederick Rutledge (1769–1821)
m. 1797
Harriott Pinckney Horry (1770–1858)

Genealogy III—The Spinster
Harriott Pinckney Horry [Rutledge]
(1770–1858)

Chapter 10

The prosperity of Hampton Plantation toward the end of the eighteenth century was due to the remarkable management ability of Harriott Pinckney Horry. Her son (now known as Charles Lucas Pinckney Horry) had remained in France with his wife Elenore whose uncle, the Marquis de Lafayette, had been imprisoned during the French Revolution. So young Horry found himself much involved with his European family ties. His association with Hampton as legal owner for forty-three years had been in name only and at his death, in 1828, the estate reverted to his mother. Mrs. Horry and her daughter (also named Harriott Pinckney Horry) were responsible for the operation and maintenance of this country seat characterized by some as more like a community. Hampton was completely self sufficient, having close to five hundred slaves, a percentage of which were trained in occupations necessary for the support of the plantation's every need. There were wheelwrights, carpenters, masons, shoemakers, etc., as well as the household servants and a multitude of workers for the rice fields. There was a completeness about Hampton which concealed the absence of a master/owner.

Mrs. Horry soon became convinced that her daughter Harriott would remain a spinster, a term used for any young girl who was not wed by age sixteen. So by 1797 she began to build a plantation house east of Hampton on the South Santee as a home for twenty-seven-year-old Harriott. With legal ownership of Hampton belonging to the Horry son, it was logical to believe that the daughter would need a home of her own. Named Harrietta, it is magnificent in every detail, directly faces its fields, and by design has carefully spaced windows and doors to provide the best cross-ventilation. False apertures are used to achieve balance. The entrance and garden side porticoes with their squared columns are actually piazza-styled, expanded porches following the trend of using Adam detail wooden variations.

Despite the unprecedented beauty of Harrietta, this plantation dream home was never occupied permanently by a member of the builder's family. Charles Lucas Pinckney Horry's decision to remain in France was followed closely by the unexpected marriage of his maiden sister, Harriott, to Frederick Rutledge (third son of "Dictator John" Rutledge). After the romantic couple eloped October 11, 1797, they

53

made their home at Hampton and therefore Harrietta was not finished. In 1828, at the death of Charles Lucas Pinckney Horry, work was begun once again on the interior of Harrietta. This time it was intended as a home for Harriott and Frederick Rutledge's son, Edward Cotesworth. He married Rebecca Motte Lowndes in 1829 and only stayed a short time at Harrietta. It was his decision to resume a naval career and his brother, the second Frederick Rutledge, was needed at Hampton. Work on Harrietta was again interrupted. The house remained unoccupied until its sale in 1858 to Stephen Doar who repaired Harrietta and lived there. So it was that (except for a brief period) this South Santee mansion remained empty for sixty years. During that time the Pinckney/Horry/Rutledge families planted rice on the Harrietta land but there was no owner/overseer living there for any length of time.

Events during the close of the eighteenth century were of great significance to life at Hampton Plantation because Harriott Horry's brothers were prominent in the political affairs of America. While Thomas Pinckney was still in London he was placed on the Federalist ticket as candidate for vice-president with John Adams. He returned to the United States to learn that Adams had won the presidency by three electoral votes and Thomas Jefferson, the vice-presidency with sixty-eight votes. Thomas Pinckney had been third with fifty-nine votes. He was then elected to Congress (September 4, 1797) from the Charleston district and planned to strengthen his Federalist party in South Carolina. His marriage on October 19, 1797, to Frances Motte Middleton (widow of John Middleton and younger sister of Thomas' beloved Betsey) brought much happiness to his life. In addition to Fairfield and Eldorado plantations, they built a handsome London-style home on George Street in Charleston.

Thomas and Charles Cotesworth Pinckney had served their country during a time of great turmoil in foreign relations. The war between France and England in 1793 had placed America in a most unfortunate situation. The United States had certain obligations to the French government for help received during the American Revolution, but it also needed to keep a peaceful trade relationship with England. This balancing act was the enormous responsibility entrusted to the Pinckney brothers by President Washington.

Thomas Pinckney returned to the United States just as his brother, Charles Cotesworth, undertook an almost impossible mission to France. As part of his official legation Charles Cotesworth secured the services of Henry Middleton Rutledge (twenty-one-year-old son of his brother-in-law, Edward Rutledge). In 1792, following the death of Henrietta Middleton Rutledge, Edward had married Mary Shubrick Eveleigh, widow of Colonel Nicholas Eveleigh, and had continued to practice law in Charleston with Charles Cotesworth. Edward's children remained much attached to the Pinckneys: His daughter Sarah lived in London with her Uncle Thomas and his family; and, following his study with Professor Cochrane at Columbia University in New York, his son Henry served as secretary to his Uncle Charles Cotesworth's legation to France. Henry had been visiting his sister in London at the time of his appointment. On August 2, 1796, Edward Rutledge wrote Henry concerning his decision to join the mission:

August 2, 1796

My dearest Henry,
    I wrote you on the 30th. ult. informing you of your Uncle Pinckney's appointment to a place of honorable importance in Europe....In times like these, I should blush, if the crest of my young Henry was not brightened by honor, and his hours perpetually devoted to active Virtue! The means are placed within your reach; you stand on a commanding eminence, avail yourself of the advantages which are now afforded you, and you may easily become an excellent Lawyer, and an able politician. A confidential Secretary to so near a relation, and to so excellent a Friend, and that in a Republic, so peculiarly circumstanced as France; will furnish opportunities of acquiring a minute knowledge of the politic's of her government, as well as of our own, and most probably of many countries of Europe. The American revolution gave rise to a new order of things in France. The French revolution has given rise to a new order of things in Europe; You will be on the Theatre of public Life, from whence you will mark the progressive changes, and by a cool and steady attention discover what occurrences arise, which may be turned to the advantage of your own country: or if no benefits can be drawn from their conduct, a knowledge of their circumstances, may enable you to avert some evils, from your own States....This is the season, my Son for improvement—surrounded by genius; in the midst of the arts and sciences; selected from among your countrymen at the age of one and twenty, by him, who in a time of peril has been himself selected, to fill so important a station—chosen as he has been with a view to unite all parties; placed as you will be under the

Edward Rutledge (1749–1800). Oil Painting by Annie Rowan Forney Daugette of an original portrait by Earle.

roof of my Friend, and directed in your studies by his wisdom; how does my heart dilate with joy, and how are my hopes excited.—dilated and excited in favor of a Son, whom I love, and admire, with the fondest affection, and who is deserving of all the affection I can bestow....I have at present nothing more to add, than to commend you, as

I sincerely do to the God of our Fathers, hoping and trusting, that he will confirm you on all virtuous habits, enlighten you with all true wisdom; adorn you with bright and luminous qualities; establish you as the protector of innocence—the defender of justice, and the firm friend of human nature, that you may experience through life, those blessings, which usually flow in upon a character, formed by such a constellation of excellence, and that your children, and your children's children may partake of the rich portion of your virtues.

God! bless you—Your affectionate Father

Ed: Rutledge

Henry traveled from London to Paris in December 1796 to begin his duties with the official party which was headquartered at the Hotel des Tuileries, Rue St. Honoré.

The policy followed by Charles Cotesworth in France was an attempt at neutrality and was completely rejected by the French Directory. This first mission to France, followed by the more famous "XYZ" mission, greatly affected political attitudes at home. Party differences were more visible now that foreign policy was an issue. With the election of John Adams in 1797 as the second president of the United States, the Federalists were anxious to maintain power equal to the Washington/Adams coalition. Edward Rutledge became governor of South Carolina in 1800 on the Federalist ticket. The Pinckney/Rutledge influence in the South had helped the Federalist cause in spite of growing criticism by the Democratic-Republicans. It was this southern support that gave Charles Cotesworth Pinckney a place in the presidential election in 1800 and made him the Federalist presidential candidate in 1804 and 1808.

A letter from Eleanor Parke Lewis (granddaughter of Mrs. George Washington) written May 9, 1801, from Mount Vernon to Mary Stead Pinckney, gives some idea of the respect for Charles Cotesworth:

> ...The regard of Genl Pinckney and yourself is allways [sic] remember'd and mention'd with pride and pleasure, and I assure you with sincerity that you have not more zealous admirers in the world than are to be met with at this time at Mount Vernon....For Genl Pinckney's *own* comfort I should never wish him to be a President, happiness I am sure is not attendant on that situation. I am persuaded he is far happier in his present employments, but for his country I think the loss is irreparable for the present four years,—after that term expires, I trust America will retrieve her character by electing him unamiously and for life....I hope indeed nothing will prevent you from visiting Mount Vernon—Grandmama will rejoice to see you....

Though unsuccessful in his bid for the office of president of the United States, Charles Cotesworth remained a strong, well-respected influence in the American political arena.

In October 1799 Governor Edward Rutledge's son Henry married his sixteen-year-old cousin, Septima Sexta Middleton, who had been born at Middleton Place, October 15, 1783, the seventh child, sixth daughter of Mary Izard and Arthur Middleton. Governor Rutledge was pleased that his son had married a Middleton woman just as he had done. Septima was a delightful conversationalist and hostess and Charleston society quickly welcomed the young couple. Henry's work with his Uncle Pinckney in the mission to France had been just the background needed for joining the Pinckney/Rutledge law firm in Charleston. Henry and Septima's close association with their aunt, Harriott Pinckney Horry, and with cousins Harriott and Frederick Rutledge, brought much happiness to family gatherings at Hampton Plantation and Middleton Place as well.

However, the death of their beloved George Washington, in December 1799, only foreshadowed the sorrow to come with the turn of the century. On January 23, 1800, Governor Edward Rutledge died of a stroke while in office. The death of his brother, "Dictator John," the state's first governor, occurred six months later. South Carolinians mourned the deaths of these two brothers. Their lives had been interwoven with the birth of their state, as well as the securing of freedom for the young nation. Their descendants would figure prominently in the life of Hampton Plantation and, fittingly, its eventual ownership by the state of South Carolina.

Chapter 11

Harriott and Frederick Rutledge had eight children by 1810. They were: Edward Cotesworth; Frederick; Elizabeth Pinckney; Harriott Pinckney; Maria; Thomas Pinckney; John Henry; and Eliza Lucas. A letter from Frederick to Harriott mentions little Edward Cotesworth just before he was six months old:

Orangeburgh April 11, 1799

My Dear Harriott,

Mr. Folkes has this moment come into the Court House to inform us that he is on his way to Charleston & asks for the commands of the Lawyers. I have therefore only time to let you hear from myself that I am well. We are actively employed in business—the Court will adjourn tomorrow *certainly* & I know of nothing which can prevent my being with you on Sunday evening, in the mean time let me entreat you to take care of yourself. I hope Edward amuses you very well. Don't let him forget either to kiss or to pray—this letter is short *only* because I have not more than time sufficient to assure you my great & unalterable love

Adieu my dearest friend & believe
me ever and entirely your's
Fred^k Rutledge

In the next year Frederick's father and uncle died leaving the Rutledge cousins more attached than ever to Mrs. Horry and her brothers, Thomas and Charles Cotesworth Pinckney. Eleanor Parke Lewis always mentioned Frederick and Harriott, as well as the Miss Pinckneys, in her letters to Mary Stead Pinckney. News from Hampton Plantation was of importance to George Washington's widow at Mount Vernon. For this reason her granddaughter, Eleanor Lewis, always made inquiry and requested that Mrs. Pinckney write often. Harriott and Frederick had two sons—Edward Cotesworth (b. Oct. 16, 1798) and Frederick (b. Oct. 28, 1800) when Eleanor Lewis wrote Mary Pinckney in May 1801:

...I am very happy to hear my amiable friends Mrs. F Rutledge, and the Miss Pinckneys are well. Mr. John Rutledge [Frederick's brother]

Rutledge Coat of Arms.

told me of Harriott's sweet little Boys, I should be much gratified with
seeing them....Be so good as to present the most affectionate regards
of Grandmama and myself to Mrs. Horry, Mrs. T. Pinckney, Mrs.
Rutledge and Miss Pinckneys—accept for yourself and General Pinckney, my Husband's and Brother's united to Grandmama's and mine
And believe me Dear and respected Mrs. Pinckney, your affectionate
Grateful and obliged

Eleanor Parke Lewis

Much can be learned of life in Charleston and at Hampton Plantation
in the early years of the nineteenth century through the reading of family
letters. Thomas Pinckney's son, Thomas Pinckney, Jr., wrote to his first
cousin, Harriott Pinckney (daughter of Charles Cotesworth), on a regular basis.

Miss Harriott Pinckney
Hampton

Charleston Dec. 22ᵈ 1801

You will receive this, My Dear Harriott, by my Mother, who to her great joy, is enabled to leave Town tomorrow. Cotesworth's fever has quite left him, and Edward is as well as ever he was....The Legislature broke up on Saturday last, and several of the Members are already in Town.—I do not know when my Uncle and Aunt & Eliza are to proceed to Santee, but I understand that Sally Rutledge is to be of their party, when they do go.—

It is rumoured in Town that Miss Shubricks wedding is to be uncommonly brilliant. The Colonel's new furniture is to be paraded on the occasion, and the Brides costume is, (I am told by the universal chronicle, Miss Hannah Drayton) inconceivably Elegant. The happy Man is to accompany Mrs. Martin when she comes. The Bride is sitting for her picture at Malbone's. It is said she coughed three times in Church last Sunday, and sneezed just as she was stepping in the carriage. You see how the minutest circumstances concerning her become of importance now.

Pearson has returned to this country, and looks as charming and keen-edged as ever. I do not know what stay he will make, but I shall endeavour to bring him to Santee some of these days. I do not know whether Mess. Grant & Guillet will remain till the races, but Report says you will have Beaux in abundance at that time.

I have been several times both to Tradd St. & Broad St. in search of letters for you, but unsuccessfully. Should I get any, they shall be forwarded with all possible dispatch.

I tender to you the Homage of my high respect & consideration—

Thomas Pinckney

This young generation of cousins seemed to be totally preoccupied with parties, races, and courting. Weddings were much anticipated social events and a missed opportunity to slip a note to a dear one in the country was a major loss. Again Thomas wrote to Harriott:

Decʳ 23th. 1801.

I rose early this morning to put my plan into execution but the violence of the rain prevented me—I am just returned from the office & I met Fredk. Rutledge in Town. oh Harriott! how could you let such an opportunity escape. Not a single line nor even a message....

On January 2, 1802, Thomas continued his correspondence with Harriott:

> I have this moment received you kind letter My Dear Cousin, and sit down immediately to atone for my impatience.—I assure you, I am truly contrite for my impetuosity, and for supposing, even for one moment, that you would withhold from me information which you knew was of the last importance to me.—But how could I divine that such a number of unlucky events should take place?—and when I saw two or three fine opportunities escape, what could I suppose but the the merriments of Christmas, & the agreement of the country, had quite driven me from your memory?—Forgive me! I will sin no more.—

But inevitably, death intruded into the happy lives centered around Hampton Plantation. Harriott Pinckney Horry Rutledge lost her beloved husband Frederick who was buried in St. Michael's church yard with this inscription marking his grave:

> Beneath this stone
> lie the earthly remains of
> FREDERICK RUTLEDGE
> who died on the 12th. of April 1821.
> age 53 years.
>
> The tenor of his whole life affords
> to his bereaved family and friends
> the well grounded hope that his
> Almighty Creator and Redeemer
> will reward in a better State those
> virtues which caused him to be so
> truly beloved
> in life, and in death
> so sincerely lamented.

Once again, women and children were predominantly in charge of Hampton, as Charles Lucas Pinckney Horry continued to live in Paris. However, the oldest Rutledge son, Edward Cotesworth, who had entered the Navy sometime before 1815, and his brother Frederick, who was twenty-one when the first Frederick died, soon began to help their mother and grandmother with the plantations. Also Thomas Pinckney aided his sister, Harriott Horry, and the newly widowed Harriott

Rutledge with the management of the Santee plantations. He wrote his sister in March of 1822:

> ...I would take as many of the hands as are necessary...to put Harrietta swamp into as complete order as the season yet admit....I would then leave with Johnson as many of the women as should ensure the crop being attended in the highest order, & I would return all the men & as many women as might not be wanted at Harrietta to Wambaw & Hampton, where they should be steadily employed through the summer in putting the Island in order....I would find two good ploughs at least to be worked by oxen to trench plough the whole of the planting land through the summer which would entirely renew the soil for the next crop...

By 1824 Edward Cotesworth Rutledge was able to return to South Carolina and spend some time with his uncle, Charles Cotesworth, on Pinckney Island near Hilton Head. One of the worst hurricanes ever to strike the Santee region (1822) had left much anxiety over weather conditions. A letter, dated September 15, 1824, from Edward Cotesworth to his mother, Harriott Rutledge, was to reassure her of their safety during a recent storm.

E.C. Rutledge.—24

> It blew very fresh about 1-o'clock this morning with a very high tide My Dear Mother. I had the house well secured, and as the sailors say, weathered the gale very well....Uncle Pinckney is again pretty well. Adieu—my love to Grandmother, and Sisters.
>
> Ever your affectionate
> Son ECR

In April 1825, fifty years after the Marquis de Lafayette had assisted the patriots in their cause against England, the remarkable French general made a triumphal tour of the United States. In Charleston he was received by his long-time friends, generals Thomas and Charles Cotesworth Pinckney in full regimental dress for the occasion. Charles Cotesworth was then president general of the Society of the Cincinnati, the fraternity which had maintained a bond between the French general and officers of the Continental army. In this capacity Charles Cotesworth delivered an address of welcome. Then Lafayette spoke of his joy in seeing those with whom he had served in the cause of freedom for America. Along with the grandness which keynoted the celebrations held for Lafayette, his personal moments with the Pinckneys were filled with family reminiscences, for Lafayette's niece was wed to the Pinckney brothers' nephew and a son-in-law of Thomas Pinckney, Francis Kinloch Huger, had liberated Lafayette from the fortress Olmutz in Moravia. Later Huger was imprisoned, Lafayette recaptured, and final liberation came in 1797 from Napoleon. Huger was with the entourage in Charleston and the grateful Lafayette had greeted the Pinckneys as brothers.

This was the last public appearance for Charles Cotesworth Pinckney. He died in August and Thomas succeeded him as president general of the Society of the Cincinnati. Thomas died in Charleston, November 2, 1828. That same year Charles Lucas Pinckney Horry died, as did the oldest daughter of Harriott Rutledge, Elizabeth Pinckney Rutledge. In 1830, death came for the sister of Thomas and Charles Cotesworth, Harriott Pinckney Horry, dead at age eighty-two. Now Harriott Pinckney Horry Rutledge became the legal owner of Hampton and the surrounding plantations of the Santee. She had survived her parents, her brother and his family, her husband, and her oldest daughter.

Part IV

THE PLANTER

Frederick Rutledge (1800–1884)

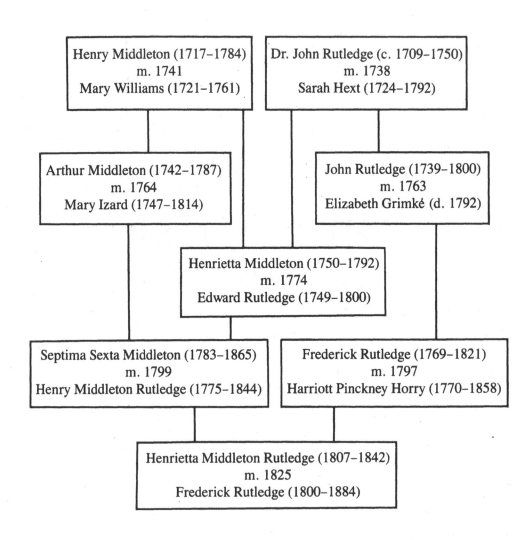

Henry Middleton (1717–1784)
m. 1741
Mary Williams (1721–1761)

Dr. John Rutledge (c. 1709–1750)
m. 1738
Sarah Hext (1724–1792)

Arthur Middleton (1742–1787)
m. 1764
Mary Izard (1747–1814)

John Rutledge (1739–1800)
m. 1763
Elizabeth Grimké (d. 1792)

Henrietta Middleton (1750–1792)
m. 1774
Edward Rutledge (1749–1800)

Septima Sexta Middleton (1783–1865)
m. 1799
Henry Middleton Rutledge (1775–1844)

Frederick Rutledge (1769–1821)
m. 1797
Harriott Pinckney Horry (1770–1858)

Henrietta Middleton Rutledge (1807–1842)
m. 1825
Frederick Rutledge (1800–1884)

Genealogy IV—The Planter
Frederick Rutledge
(1800–1884)

Chapter 12

For the last two years of her life, Harriott Horry had been assisted at Hampton not only by her daughter but also by her two oldest Rutledge grandsons. At her death their roles became more important than ever. Hampton remained fully active and inhabited by several generations of owners and servants alike. It was not uncommon for a plantation household to have the following: A housekeeper; her assistant; a "mauma" in charge of the children and as many nursery maids as there were boys and girls in the house; a seamstress; a clearstarcher; a cook with a girl in training and a boy to help her; many laundresses; a butler and one or more footmen; a body-servant for each gentleman; and a coachman with as many grooms and stable boys as were needed for the number of horses kept. The assistants were usually the children of the older servants. Their pride in their work was passed from one generation to the next and these positions were jealously guarded.

There is evidence throughout the Hampton correspondence that the owners were compassionate and just in their dealings with their servants. During a brief period when Lieutenant Edward Cotesworth Rutledge was planting at Harrietta, his brother Frederick wrote him concerning their treatment of a certain slave named Paul:

> My dear Edward
>
> Patty seems to be very much distressed about Paul—leaving her out of the case, I think that his punishment has been sufficient for his offence—I am always anxious to keep my word even to the most humble. I told Paul some time since that if he behaved himself well he should be replaced, his having passed to your orders has prevented me from doing so. I would willingly supply his place in the field by one of my own hands & I have been deterred from making the offer solely by the belief that it would not be acceptable—I have taken the trouble to put this on paper in order that you may see that the value of my promise in this instance depends upon yourself—
>
> Your very aff^e Brother
Fred—⊥ Rutledge

Hampton
15th Dec^r

From 1825 until 1834 Frederick Rutledge appears to have been directly responsible for Hampton. It was in 1825 that Frederick married
his cousin, Henrietta Middleton Rutledge, of Nashville, Tennessee. The
wedding was held in Nashville on her parents' twenty-sixth anniversary
(Septima and Henry Rutledge had been wed in South Carolina on Septima's sixteenth birthday, October 15, 1799). The Nashville ceremony
united the granddaughter of Arthur Middleton and Edward Rutledge
(South Carolina signers of the Declaration of Independence) with the
grandson of John Rutledge (first governor of South Carolina). Henrietta
had migrated to Tennessee with her family in 1816.

Septima Sexta Middleton and Henry Middleton Rutledge had married
while Henry's father, Edward, was governor of South Carolina. Edward
died in office three months later and Henry was immediately left with the
responsibilities of his father's law partnership with Charles Cotesworth
Pinckney. Charles Cotesworth treated Henry like the son he never had as
their years together in the American legation to France had strengthened
their bonds of affection and respect. A typical part of their relationship
was revealed in a letter from Charles Cotesworth to Henry:

Santee Feb ʳʸ 15ᵗʰ 1812

Dear Henry,

    I have just received a Letter from M:ʳ Kershaw, mentioning that you
had called & settled with him....Now I know you have made a very bad
Crop; & I am well acquainted with the low price of Cotton; I therefore
enclose you a check on the South Carolina Bank for the sum you have
paid M:ʳ Kershaw, & request you to do me the favour to let it remain
unpaid, till you make a good Crop....

Your affectionate uncle

Charles Cotesworth Pinckney

My daughters unite with me in love to Septima, you & your children &
we all hope we shall see you both, & as many of the children as you can
bring with you, in the spring at the Island—we shall be there the end of
this month.

Henry and Septima Rutledge were well admired by the Pinckneys and the respect was mutual among the Middleton/Rutledge/Pinckney family members.

Henry's father, Edward Rutledge, had bought a large block of land grants from his elder brother, John, to help him financially. The Revolution had stripped many patriots of resources and recovery had been difficult, even for "Dictator John." When Edward died the land grants did not automatically become Henry's because the laws of primogeniture were no longer valid. For this reason Henry purchased his own inheritance for a nominal sum. These original North Carolina land grants were now a part of the new state of Tennessee, so Henry Rutledge traveled to Tennessee in 1807, where he surveyed and registered in his name over 73,000 acres of land. He contracted to build a magnificent country home on the Elk River in Franklin County. In 1816 he brought his wife and five children, twenty wagons of belongings, and fifty slaves to the boarded, painted mansion they called Chilhowee. By 1820 the family had built Rose Hill, a fine town house and twenty-acre estate in the much-desired area near the University of Nashville. Henry Rutledge became a member of the Davidson County bar, a well-respected citizen, and was the official escort/interpreter for Lafayette's entourage during the general's visit to Nashville in 1825. In the same tradition of the South Carolina low-country planters, the Rutledge family divided their time between Chilhowee and Rose Hill, with trips home to Middleton Place as often as possible to renew family ties and to introduce the Rutledge daughters into Charleston society. There Henrietta came to know and love her handsome cousin, Frederick Rutledge of Hampton Plantation, resulting in the union of the two Rutledge branches.

Chapter 13

Life at Hampton Plantation for Henrietta and Frederick Rutledge was a mixture of happiness and struggle as Frederick sought to adjust to the responsibilities of a planter. It was a difficult period of change for the great rice plantations. In the 1820s there was a general economic decline in Charleston and other southern port cities. Bitter rivalries with the ports to the north developed, with New York being the victor. By 1808 foreign slave trade had ended, international commerce had been affected by an embargo, and the emphasis on industry in New England had lessened the need for southern economic support. Even the boom in prices for sea-island cotton between 1815 and 1819 failed to make Charleston the principal cotton port as she had been for the rice trade. While Savannah, her neighbor to the south, experimented with "steam" instead of "sail" by sending the steamship *Savannah* under Captain Moses Rogers across the Atlantic, Charleston fell behind. Her merchants could not compete and the attempts to modernize transportation facilities and methods were unsuccessful. This change increased costs to the planters and Frederick Rutledge endeavored to increase the production of the family plantations.

During this time resorts in the North began to attract the low-country planters. It had become undesirable to stay on the rice plantations during the summer months because of the threat of "country fever." It was now known that the stagnant, flooded rice fields and marshes provided perfect breeding areas for disease-carrying mosquitoes. From May 10 until November 15 each year the South Carolina planters and their families retreated to the islands, moved into the "High Hills of the Santee," journeyed to the "up country" near Greenville, or migrated to the spas and springs at Newport, Rhode Island, Saratoga, New York, or other popular health and recreational sites in the Carolinas and Virginia. Sullivan's Island had been a longtime summer resort for Charlestonians who thought it beneficial to escape the danger of intermittent epidemics of yellow fever. Newport had been a resort area for wealthy southern colonists as early as 1765 and, following the Revolution, experienced an increase in its popularity along with that of Saratoga Springs. In the summer of 1826 Henrietta and Frederick were among the South Carolina low-country planters visiting Saratoga as fellow guests of Chris-

Photo—R. Alan Powell
Courtesy—Owner, Benjamin Bosworth Smith,
Charleston, South Carolina.

Photo—Jim Wheeler
Courtesy—Benjamin Bosworth Smith,
Charleston, South Carolina.

Henrietta Middleton Rutledge
Rutledge (1807–1842). Detail of
portrait thought to be painted
c. 1841–1842 by Samuel Osgood.

Frederick Rutledge (1800–1884),
artist unknown, painted c. 1825.

topher Jenkins of Edisto Island. Henrietta's family from Tennessee was
there for the season staying at the grandest of all resort hotels, the United
States Hotel, which had opened in 1824.

Tragedy struck the happy group of vacationers with the deaths of Henrietta's two-year-old brother Cotesworth Pinckney and four-year-old sister Helen. The cause of their deaths is not recorded, only that they were
buried in Saratoga Springs. Henrietta's twenty-four-year-old brother
Edward Augustus, severely depressed and weakened by an illness he had
suffered the winter before, shot and killed himself on July 16 and was
buried with the younger Rutledge children. In another few short years
Henrietta and Frederick experienced the loss of their first-born, a son
Edward, followed by the trauma of yet another suicide in the immediate
family. Frederick's youngest brother, John Henry, killed himself at
Hampton in March 1830. There is an account of his death written by
Thomas Pinckney's granddaughter, ten-year-old Mary Esther Huger,
when she was visiting Charleston from Pendleton, South Carolina:

> Whilst we were there, we heard of a young man shooting himself dying
> in a short time. We did not know him, but he was our Cousin John
> Rutledge who killed himself because a druggist refused to let him
> marry his pretty daughter, as Mrs. Rutledge had told him, however
> good his child might be, it would be impossible to receive her into her

family—which he probably expected & thought right—as social lines were more strong then. I have heard that the young man lived long enough to repent his violence. He is buried in the garden at Hampton on Santee River....

His gravestone bears the following inscription:

In Memory
of
John Henry Rutledge
Son of
Frederick and Harriott (Horry) Rutledge
who departed this life
on the 5th of March 1830
aged 21 years
He was distinguished for
Fortitude & firmness
The Goodness & the magnanimity that he
showed even in the agonies of a painful
Death made indelible impressions upon
all who witnessed it
He died in Peace with all men & in the full
Confidence that his Maker would receive
his Soul with that Mercy & forgiveness
which is the hope & solace of the Penitent
in his approach to the throne
of the Eternal

Tragedy came often to the low-country planters—families were large and many infants died in the first month or two of life; the various fevers and infectious diseases were no respecters of age; and natural disasters took their toll on entire communities. Along with an acceptance of high mortality rates came the always unexpected shock of murder or suicide. Long periods of mourning were often interrupted by other reasons for grief so that in December 1830, Harriott Horry's death brought not only added sorrow to Hampton but heavier responsibilities to her grandson Frederick.

Chapter 14

The decade of the 1830s brought a series of changes at Hampton as Harriott Horry's grandsons, Edward Cotesworth and Frederick Rutledge, were not particularly adept at plantation management. Edward preferred his naval career and Frederick became involved in an enterprising resort development that would permanently affect the pattern of summer travel for many South Carolina planters. Just before Edward Cotesworth resumed his naval voyages in August 1832, his wife Becky (Rebecca Motte Lowndes, granddaughter of Thomas Pinckney) gave birth to a daughter, Harrie (Harriott Horry). Becky and her daughter had spent most of their time at Hampton along with Frederick, Henrietta, and their two-year-old daughter Lize (Elizabeth Pinckney). An account of the cousins written in 1833 by their grandmother to Edward reads:

> Lieut' Rutledge
> U.S. Ship St. Louis
> Pensacola
> West FLorida
>
> ...I so wish my dear Son you could see Lize play with *"Harrot Horry"* as she calls your daughter, your cousin Cotesworth's [son of Thomas Pinckney] term for her is *little perfection*....Your Mother prays God to bless her own Dear Son.
>
> H.P. Rutledge

Even though she missed Edward, Harriott depended on her son Frederick to manage the plantations and realized that his task was discouraging, that his older brother was constantly on tour with the navy, and that Frederick was more excited about the development of his "little Charleston of the mountains" than about the tremendous burden of a planter's duties.

As early as 1829 Frederick purchased land in western North Carolina in an area of Buncombe County known as Flat Rock. Some three years earlier he had negotiated a purchase in nearby Limestone, North Carolina, for low-country planter Daniel Blake. The two friends, along with

Judge Mitchell King and Charles Baring, thought the area an excellent
location for a summer resort and so began the awesome challenge of
convincing other wealthy South Carolinians to build summer homes
there, rather than make the annual tour of the spas and springs to the
north. This was not an easy venture as travel by water to Newport and
other northern resorts was a simple matter compared with the ten-to-
fourteen day journey overland to the mountains. However, the healthful
atmosphere and the beauty of the natural surroundings overcame the
difficulties involved so that by the mid-1830s there was a summer community of low-country planters established at Flat Rock. In 1831 Daniel
Blake married Henrietta's sister, Emma Middleton Rutledge, from
Nashville, Tennessee, and by 1836 had built The Meadows, a permanent, two-story stone dwelling near Flat Rock. Their property in Limestone (now Fletcher) included 950 acres and was the beginning of the
Blake family's conclave in North Carolina. Henrietta and Frederick's
home, Brookland, was in Flat Rock a short distance from The Meadows.
Flat Rock soon became a lavish playground for some and a desirable
year-round residence for others. Family correspondence of the period
related the significance of this development to life at Hampton. Frederick's letters to Edward Cotesworth began to show his concern for the
plantation and March 8, 1832, he wrote:

Photo—C. E. Staton, Jr.
Courtesy—Owners, Mr. & Mrs. C. E. Staton, Jr., Flat Rock, North Carolina

Original cabin built at Brookland by Frederick Rutledge (1800–1884) in
1829—Flat Rock, North Carolina.

I rec^d your note with the enclosed directions this morning....Old William has been very sick with the influenza, he is perhaps a little better, but appears to be to use his own phrase "much worsted." I should like to know where you intend to get Seed Rice for Harrietta, there is none at Tranquillity fit Seed, when Tranquillity & Mottefield are supplied—I shall plant some of Hampton...Ed^{wd} Pinckney [Becky's uncle] to whom I showed a parcel, says that it is not fit for seed....Planting time is approaching....

For the next few years the letters to Edward Cotesworth fill in the details concerning his travels, his family, Hampton, and even the news from Flat Rock in Buncombe County:

E.L.R. [Eliza Lucas Rutledge, b. 1810]

To/Lieut^t E C Rutledge

USN.

New York.—

Charleston September 24th 1832.

My dear brother

I know you do not like reading letters in general but I am vain enough to imagine you would like to read one from *me*....I mean to take care of Becky during your absence....Becky tells me little Harriott is to be Christened the 28th of this month....I had looked forward to her being *my* godchild but since you wish both of aunts to stand I shall be satisfied to love her as a niece, as the daughter of my dear brother and of my sweet and gentle friend.—Mama got a letter from Tom [Thomas Pinckney Rutledge, their brother, who was at school in Cambridge, Massachusetts] this morning he is quite well. I long for October to pass away and for *winter* to come. It will kill the mosquitoes...and bring F [Frederick] home....Yours in haste

Ever affectionately L

R M R [Rebecca Motte Rutledge]
To/Lieut: Rutledge
U.S.N.
FORWARDED ~~New York~~
Pensacola Florida

Charleston October 5th 1832.—

You have not yet told me to direct to you any where else my dear
Edward so I still continue to write to New York....This has been a fatal
year in the country. Every body has been sick, and many have fallen
victims to the fever....I am told (with how much truth I know not,) that
Frederick has grown extremely pious, and that Henrietta has been the
means of making him so; if it is true Henrietta has great cause I am
sure for happiness and shows how much better simplicity and piety is,
than a cultivated mind without it—Oh how often, and how feverently
have I wished that I were religious! but my efforts are too feeble for me
ever to feel satisfied with myself, and though I believe that I love God,
I sometimes fear that I love you and little Ducky better. I have written
three pages, and not said one word of the darling; her beauty and
sprightiness [sic] are the admiration of all eyes, and the theme of every
tongue, and if we should all meet again, I hope that you will find her as
charming as you could desire—Tomorrow she will be 8 weeks old, and
every body pronounces her strength and liveliness to be surprising for
that age—Now this is all truth not at all vanity. I shall be more clear-
sighted to her defects than any one else.—Adieu dearest—With love
from Mama and a kiss from Ducky I remain

Your aff^{te} Wife R M R

R M R
To/Lieut. Rutledge
U.S. Ship St. Louis
Norfolk
Virginia

Charleston October 10th 1832

...You would laugh to hear what an adept I am grown in baby talk, and
you would not rail at it as foolish if you could see how she laughs and
springs at the sound of my voice.—I was put in a very moralizing mood

this morning by an advertisement in the Newspaper—*Almanacs for 1833* I suddenly remembered that this year must pass away, and another and another, and finally that Time to each individual is the beginning of Eternity, and then the drowsy trifling manner in which most people, but myself particularly allow this most precious of God's gifts to slip through their hands unmarked by one good thing—and then—the actual necessity of improving our Time, for the promotion of our *temporal* happiness alone, and other commonplace ideas…made me sad for a while, but did no manner of good, such a hardened sinner am I!

Our mothers's family is as usual…They all look forward to Frederick's arrival with pleasure, but I do not think that will be before the middle of November, for Etta's *second* Daughter was born only the 26th of the last month—its name I suppose be *Septima* [Sarah Henrietta Rutledge, born at Brookland in Flat Rock].

Adieu dear Edward

Your's Ever R M R

R M R
Lieut: Rutledge
U.S. Ship St. Louis
Pensacola
West Florida

El Dorado April 10th 1833

….Miss Maria Middleton is engaged to be married to Mr Edward Pringle, they are enjoying the Romance of their young Love at Middleton Place, and I suppose will be married this Spring—it is a match which the world generally approves, and it appears to me to be…a suitable one.—[Maria Henrietta Middleton was the daughter of Mary Helen Hering and Henry Middleton (South Carolina Governor, 1810–1812; Minister to Russia, 1820–1830; son of Arthur Middleton, signer of the Declaration of Independence)]. All your Mother's family except Tom and yourself will soon be assembled at Hampton, for Dr. Holbrook and cousin Harriott [Edward's brother-in-law and sister] are on their way there now….M[Edward's sister Maria] did speak of going to Buncombe with Frederick but she appears to have changed her mind—I wish you too were at home for indeed we all want you, and it is so long since I have heard from you—your little daughter wants you, for she calls pa-pa-pa-pa very loudly—but not loud enough alas to reach across the Sea.—She will be eight months old day after tomorrow and is pretty and sweet—but Frederick's Sally far surpasses her in size....

El Dorado May 15th 1833

....Henrietta, & Frederick accompanied by your sister Maria left Hampton for Buncombe on the 11th. Henrietta was sick in body and mind, she suffers a great deal on account of her sister Mrs. Blake who is in miserable health...The only person now at Santee besides ourselves is...Dr. Smith. We have been waiting a very long time for the arrival of Captain Kerrison to take us to Town...we have determined to wait no longer but go by land....Your mother...was very kind in offering to take me down with her, and I fear I did what she disapproved of in remaining; but the country is so cool, and the air in Town so filled with...Scarlet fever...I preferred staying as long as I could....

Charleston 3rd June 1833

My dear husband—It is near three weeks since I have written to you, at that time I was still in the country and lest you should feel uneasy respecting our late sojourn there I hasten to inform you that we have all been in town the required time and are all as yet quite safe from country fever—....

Charleston June 14th 1833

....We are all agape with admiration of the steam-packet, which runs now between New York and this place....It makes about three trips a month, and weathers a storm in safety....I am thinking of this steamboat with particular complacency as a means of conveying us safely to you should you arrive in...New York...for you know I am courageous and afraid of nothing but a cow—Alas Alas!!....till then believe in the constant affection of your wife

R M Rutledge.—

Edward's return to South Carolina prompted the following letter from Frederick:

Buncombe County NC
2^d of Sep^R 1833

My dear Brother,

Your safe return to your family is the most agreeable intelligence that I have rec^d this summer from Charleston. You must enjoy *home, Sweet home* again, from which an absence was necessary to make you know its value—your stay will I hope be more permanent than usual, & that you are more inclined to plough the fields, than to plough the deep. I wish you better success than I have experienced—After a slavery of eight years to a planters duties, I am worse off than when I began—I am now aware (that situated as I am in the lower Country) one or two years more of my present system of planting w^d complete my ruin—but I do not intend to cease struggling (I have had nothing else since my return to America) & will not succumb to the difficulties and untoward circumstances of my life. In a paper which my dear father wrote, a few days before his death, he said "I *wish* my son Frederick to remain in Carolina & devote himself to his mother—" that wish has been complied with. I shall not enumerate my services or my sacrifices, but only regret that my efforts did not by half equal my wishes to promote the interests of the family of the Dearest & kindest of parents—whose removal from this world *I feel* more & more every year and every day of my life. It is now time for me to attempt to make some provision for those, whose first & only claims are upon me....

Frederick continued by reporting on crops at Harrietta and Mottefield and offered to visit the Santee plantations with Edward in November in order to review the situation there. He told Edward that the Flat Rock area had been "very populous this summer" but that he had been alone because Henrietta was in Tennessee. He mentioned seeing no one "except Mr Barring" whose advice he respected as "there is much that is estimable in his character, & his knowledge is of the practical & useful sort." Charles and Susan Baring had become the most prominent of the early founders of the Flat Rock community. Their estate, Mountain Lodge, included a mansion of splendid proportions with grounds landscaped following the pattern of an English country seat. Their beautiful brick chapel-of-ease, St. John in the Wilderness, soon became the established Episcopal church for communicants in the entire area. The Barings' friendship with Frederick and Henrietta was an influencing factor in the decision to give up plantation life as was the more healthful atmosphere in the Cherokee Indians' "land of the sky." Frederick's letter to his brother was solemn and determined as he closed by sending his love to Becky and saying that he doubted if Henrietta would return to Hampton:

> ....I do not wish her to do so—at least not this winter—If she was here she would send her love to you. Lize remembers you & talks very often of her little Cousin H & Sarah is yet to be introduced to you....believe me, Your aff^t brother & sincere friend—
>
> > Fred^k Rutledge

Harriott Rutledge was now to be aided in the management of the plantations by Edward Cotesworth. In January 1835 she wrote him from Hampton concerning certain slaves and the planting season to come:

> As the weather is once more mild ole Sandy is anxious to begin his services for you, and therefore goes to town this evening....I have a young Lad about 15 years old, well disposed, a brother of Tom who I gave to Harriott and I have had him taught to plough....I rely on him to do you some good. I wish to send you a deed of gift for these people Sandy and Sabey (for Life is as we well know most uncertain)....

By March of that same year the uncertainty which Edward's mother mentioned had entered their lives—threatened war with Mexico took Edward away from his planter's duties and letters to him were addressed: U.S. Frigate *Constitution*, New York. The women at Hampton took this separation very hard yet they managed, as the generations before them, to see that the planting was done. Harriott wrote her son:

> ....Becky spoke to old Sandy while I was there, and arranged with him to attend to Every thing and he is to start Sabey on the plough this afternoon....Adieu my Son I will not pain you by saying how bitter to me is your absence but I pray for you with all the truest love of
>
> > Your own dear Mother
> >
> > Harriott P. Rutledge

Edward had returned to Charleston by summer 1837 because there is a letter from Henrietta begging him to come to Flat Rock for his health:

> We are all much concerned to hear that you have a troublesome cough though you choose to make light of it. I join my entreaties with Daniel, Emma & Fred^k that you should try our mountain breezes....in this pleasant Season you may easily regain y^r health....

Frederick's relationship with his family and with Hampton was by no means ended. There had been feelings of failure but they seemed no greater then the problems Edward had caused due to his own long periods of absence. As time passed the two brothers seemed more and more to share the responsibility of helping their mother. In some ways Frederick would always be a planter.

Chapter 15

As the year 1838 began auspiciously for the Middleton/Rutledge/ Pinckney families, lives were no longer centered around Charleston and the great rice plantations. Travel conditions had improved and westward expansion had dispersed the permanent residential locations of many family members. However, there was a general tendency to winter in Charleston, when possible, as visits to the plantations were unsafe at any other season. Henry and Septima Rutledge brought their Tennessee family to Middleton Place for Christmas 1837 and remained in Charleston for the 1838 social season. Septima had two very good reasons to visit South Carolina that winter as both her daughters, Henrietta and Emma, were expecting babies and would undoubtedly need her assistance. Although Henrietta had three healthy youngsters (Lize would soon be eight, Sally was five, and Edward was almost two), her first son named Edward had died in 1829 at birth. Emma's first child, Daniel Henry Blake, had been born in Nashville and had lived only from June 15 until August 13, 1832, complicating her health and state of mind. Just three years later Henrietta's nine-month-old son, Frederick Henry, had died in Greenville, South Carolina, and was buried in the small graveyard at Christ Church.

There were friends and family members living in Greenville during part of the sickly season each year and some even had established permanent homes there. The Reverend Charles Cotesworth Pinckney (grandson of Thomas Pinckney, 1750–1828) was the first rector of Christ Church in Greenville, serving from 1835–1846, and sharing his time there with the congregation at St. James Santee. Frederick and Henrietta were frequent visitors in this resort village, for by this time a tri-weekly stage connected Asheville and Charleston with regular stops in Flat Rock, Greenville, and Columbia. Henry and Mary Helen Middleton had a Greenville summer home, Whitehall, from 1813–1820 on land he had bought from Elias Earle in 1813. Whitehall had been a convenient stopover for Middleton family members traveling in the area. Later, lengthy correspondence had been the only visitation for family members during the ten years Henry Middleton was minister to Russia (1820–1830). During that time family news from Chilhowee, Rose Hill, Brookland, The Meadows, Middleton Place, and Hampton filled the letters between Septima Rutledge and Mary Helen Middleton so that now every opportunity for those members of their "dear circle" to visit in person only served to strengthen the family ties. Likewise, it was not uncommon for the women from Hampton to visit Greenville and Flat Rock on their way to the "Springs" in Virginia just as their Tennessee cousins did on their circuit through North Carolina to Charleston.

Sarah Rutledge (only daughter of Edward Rutledge) had maintained a close relationship with her brother's family in Nashville, frequently journeying with them to Philadelphia or Newport from Charleston, and was always available to nurse her niece, Emma, or to provide companionship for Becky, Harrie, and Harriott Rutledge when they traveled to Buncombe from Hampton. Aunt Sally Rutledge, who never married, cherished the years she spent as a child in London with the Pinckney families after her mother's death. As a result she devoted much of her energy and time to her Hampton cousins as well as to her own nieces and nephews.

The men who were planters did not travel extensively as did the women due to political and business obligations; yet for more and more planters a pattern of absentee ownership was developing. The family correspondence in 1838 gives insight concerning the broadening range of life-styles and the circumstances that drew a widely separated family together. Frederick Rutledge hinted at Henrietta's forthcoming delivery in a letter to his brother at Hampton:

Charleston 14th Jan^Y 1838

My dear Edward,

....We are all as we were when you left as regards the health of this family—'though as "coming events cast their shadows before" we may expect some changes very soon. I hope Harriott continues to improve by the country air, and that Becky feels better than she did. Henrietta unites with me in love to all at Hampton—

Your aff^t Brother
Frederick Rutledge

22 Jany 1838

My dear Edward,

....the only news that I have to tell is that Emma is the mother of a fine boy—he was born about 10 oclock this morning [Frederick Rutledge Blake]—Lize and Sally and Major Rutledge [Henry Middleton Rutledge] and Harriott [Mrs. Holbrook, sister of Edward and Frederick] went to the Phrenologist on Saturday & had all their bumps carefully examined—he gave them all high characters for intellectuality and morality—I wish that little Harry had been of the party—but perhaps you are all better in a comfortable country house in this bitter weather—with my love to all at Hampton

> I am sincerely
>
> Your affe brother
>
> Fre[k] Rutledge

Henrietta gave birth a few days later to a daughter, Alice Izard, and their entire entourage made a visit to Hampton in March. Harriott Rutledge, still in command of her household, wrote her instructions to her son:

> Monday March 19th 1838

I write to you from my room dear Edward where I have been a fortnight the greater part of the time in bed, if the weather moderates I shall I hope ride out tomorrow pray tell Becky that she must expect on Saturday evening Major Rutledge, with M[rs] R. Henrietta and the children and I will thank you to desire Grace to have the 2 front chambers got ready....do tell Patty that capers are in the passage closet, and in the Press in the School room; mustard in the Store room, God bless you all

> Your affect Mother
>
> H.P. Rutledge

Later that spring Edward's sister Harriott sent further news and instructions:

My dear Edward

I write for Mama who is tired & unwell tonight—the travelers have just got in—and we are glad to hear that you are coming on Saturday. Don't make it later for I will not have Harrie with me long before the journey—Mama wishes you would send Grace Peter & tailor Will to her by Kerrison who will be up in a few days....Ask maum Patty to put up the parlour carpet in leaf tobacco which we must get from George— I write in haste...

> Yrs ever affe[tly]
>
> H P H

That May, Becky, her daughter, her mother-in-law, and Aunt Sally Rutledge rode the train to Philadelphia with plans also to visit White Sulphur Springs and other resorts in Virginia later that summer for the healthful waters. Becky's letter to Edward described their first day on the train and expressed her hope that he would decide to summer in Buncombe:

....Mama and myself are not much more fatigued than we were in the morning, but Aunt Sally has gone to bed excessively weary...Harry is well and in the highest spirits—She sends you a great many loves and kisses—and also desired that a message might be written to her Mauma and Maria the servant; not very complimentary you will say to all of her relations, but in excuse 'twas by particular desire—I do not find rail road travelling particularly pleasant—The noise is to me an insufferable objection—'tis impossible to speak, or even to think, sleep was the only recourse, and all the passengers in our car slept almost continually....I hope to hear soon from you that you are staying with my cousins—

Your's aff^{ly}

R M Rutledge

Edward did not journey to the mountains but stayed in Charleston at the Tradd Street house where he received a note from Frederick who was returning to Flat Rock:

1 June 1838

Greenville SC

My dear Edward

I have just arrived here with all my family and fellow travellers (the Rev^d C C P [Pinckney] and his family) we made a good stage load—and we all love the journey better than I expected. I left a piece of business unfinished which I must request you to attend to me—viz tell Coachman Isaac to send the empty barrels...to the Cook Store of Messrs Kinloch & Mordecai. They will fill the B^s with Seed Peas for Har^a & Wat^h [Harrietta and Waterhan]....

Your aff^t Brother

Fred^k Rutledge

Travel by rail or by stage involved certain discomforts but the dangers were minimal compared with a voyage by steam packet to the northern resorts. In August 1837, on a southward voyage, the steamer *Home* had been lost off the coast of North Carolina. To abate the growing public apprehension of ocean travel, the prominent merchants of Savannah, Georgia, formed a joint stock company and commissioned the building of a stronger, faster boat for travel between Savannah and Baltimore the following season. The extreme safety of the steamship *Pulaski* was advertised well. There were two distinct innovations: a double crew, allowing ample rest between shifts; and overnight passage to Baltimore. Savannah passengers would spend the first evening in Charleston and leave early enough to breakfast the third day in Baltimore passing "only one night at sea." Three successful voyages already that year persuaded the traveling public that the *Pulaski* was ready for a reassuring, safe passage from Savannah and Charleston to the north.

Among those boarding the *Pulaski* in Charleston, June 13, 1838, never to return, were: Edward and Frederick's unmarried sister Maria Rutledge; their brother Thomas Pinckney Rutledge and his new bride Frances M. Blake [sister of Daniel]; as well as Maria Henrietta Middleton [daughter of Henry and Mary Helen Middleton] and her husband, Edward Jenkins Pringle, their child, and a servant. The weather had been perfect and the first full day at sea, uneventful. Then that evening as the passengers slept, there came the unexpected, deafening roar of the ship's boiler as it exploded. There were eyewitness accounts describing the carnage, the screams, the deaths both instant and prolonged, and the eventual rescue of only 54 of the 131 on board. Of the family from Hampton, Edward Cotesworth Rutledge was now alone in the grief-stricken city of Charleston. A letter from his sister Lu, who had joined their mother in Philadelphia, spoke of their heartbroken reactions and their longing to be with him and others of the families so devastated by the sinking of the *Pulaski:*

Philadelphia July 22ᵈ 1838.—

....We have been fortunate in getting lodgings here in the same house with Mrs. Drayton [her daughter Emma was a passenger on the *Pulaski*]... with the Draytons...she has associations of Tom! You remember the kindness they extended to him....That poor boy loved you very truly Edward; he has often spoken of you to me in terms of affection and esteem, as a man whose good opinion he valued and hoped always to retain.—Mama seems haunted with the desire now to return home. He who was to have been her traveling companion, to be "where're she turned her eyes," sleeps in his watery grave and she frequently says, "...I want to be at home!"—I had a letter from Becky two or three days ago who still goes on hoping against hope, that the loved and lost ones will be restored to us in this world....Mrs. Drayton entertains the same idea, that many who we weep over as dead may have been picked up by vessels bound to some distant port...from which they will come back to us *months hence*....Alas! this hope is vain! this expectation, feverish restlessness! It is better to acknowledge the hand of God at once. *He* gave them. He took them. They are His, not ours....It is a great comfort to me dear Edward to think that their last moments must have been unaccompanied by such dreadful suffering as might have been theirs had they lingered long on the wreck. And do you know, Tom has told me very often that he could not bear the thought of being buried in the Earth, that the thought was repulsive to him; so much that he meant one of these days to write a paper to leave in his will a request that he should be carried and let down into the stream. I used to laugh and ask him what signified whether we were food for fishes instead of food for worms. He said I might smile at his way of viewing the matter, but he would very much prefer to Mother Earth the Ocean for his grave. He has told me this *very often* and in earnest, but never seemed at all superstitious about his death. The idea of drowning never seemed to occur to him.—Oh! how I wish it had been permitted to me to spend the last few days that he was on Earth in the company of Tom and Maria! but so to go down without one parting Kiss!!!

Tomorrow...we set out for New York, and spending one day there, go to New Haven, to Providence, and so on to the Mountains. I have been there before and thought the scenery grander than any other in America.—I hope mama will take some pleasure in the sight. The air too is pure and bracing. Becky writes me word that little Harrie is better for her travels, but her own health is not better yet. Perhaps the Springs may be of some service....The more friends I lose in this world, the more I grapple to my heart those it has pleased God to spare me.—

Your affectionate

L R

Frederick wrote to Edward about the same time:

Photo—William T. Justice
Courtesy—Kellwood Company, Asheville, North Carolina

The Meadows built c. 1836 by Daniel Blake (1803–1873)—Fletcher, North
Carolina.

July 23ᵈ 1838 Buncombe

N C

My dearest Edward

I have often wished to write to you not to offer any consolation for I
know that any attempt of that kind would be irrelevant & useless—but
to assure you how sincerely I lament the awful calamity that has be-
fallen our family and many other families on the terrible 14ᵗʰ of last
month. I have not heard from My Mother since her arrival at the
north—I am afraid that 'though habituated to sorrow, she will give way
to her grief, and be more depressed by this last & heavy adversity than
ever—I know that you have some excellent friends in Charleston & I
hope that you allow them to see you often. I fear that you have too much
solitude for the present state of your feelings. Mr. Blake begs that you

will come to Murrayville [Fletcher] and live with him until your family returns from the Vir'ᵃ Sprᵍˢ. If you could be induced to come this far, you would derive Great Benefits from the fine climate and the change of Scene....I am staying at the house of an old couple...the house is very quiet & there are no other lodgers. It is only six miles from Mr. Blake's. Etta and Em have an opportunity of seeing each other occasionally. I intended to have written when Becky & Hal passed but my anxiety about poor little Alice made me postpone it. She appears a little better but is still very feeble & puny.

Let me entreat you my dear brother to remember that you have every inducement for exertion on account of your wife & child—your duties and Responsibilities as Husband & father should prevent your being so depressed by sorrow as to forget how Dependent those dear & gentle beings are whom God has given to you.

> I am most sincerely
> Your affe brother
> Fredᵏ Rutledge

A letter from Becky in August expressed her disappointment that Edward had not joined them at the Springs and mentioned the fact that Mr. Van Buren, president of the United States, was staying at their lodge, and that Harrie "says she likes the island [Pinckney Island] a great deal better than the mountains,—and wishes that I had not brought her away from you.—" His six-year-old daughter was obviously homesick by now and added this note to her mother's letter:

> My dear Papa
>
> I shall be glad to see you when I go home and I ask you why you did not come with Mʳ Ingraham. Tell Mauma Kate that I am well—Tell Maria that I have seen some Maple sugar and I will bring her some if I can get it. Tell my Godmothers that this is my third letter to my Papa
>
> Your affᵗᵉ Daughter
> H H R

As late as the third of September Lu Rutledge writes her brother Edward from Philadelphia warning him that they had heard there was yellow fever in Charleston:

> ...I think you run a great risk of taking the fever in Charleston or the Island. I hope you are going to some healthy place till the danger is

over. I daresay Frederick would be very glad to see you up in Buncombe, and Mr. Blake also; If not in that direction go any where you like better where the air is pure and wholesome.—

A letter from Edward's daughter Harrie on September 16, 1838, related the homeward circuit and must have cheered him:

> My dear Papa,
>
> I hope to see you soon—I am so tired of the journey. I wish I was at home with you—I am going to bring you here with me next Summer if I can get you to come—I am now at the Sweet Springs—we are going to the Salt Sulphur next then we shall go to the Grey and then we are going to start on our journey home, and I shall be so glad to see you.—Give each of my Godmothers a kiss for me—I am glad you kept my birthday with Mauma Kate—but how could you know any thing about the Virginia way of frying chicken without coming here—I wish heartily I was at home—I hope you do not find yourself too solitary....I am very fond of playing ten pins—I have often heard of nine pins, but never before I came to the Springs, of ten pins.—
>
> Your affectionate Daughter
>
> H H R

Becky wrote Edward from the Salt Sulphur Springs on September 17:

> ...At the Sweet Springs we were very much surprised to see Arthur Rutledge [twenty-one-year old son of Henry and Septima Rutledge] he came there expressly to see his Aunt [Sally Rutledge, his father's sister], and remained with her two days and then went on to Washington to deliver up his accounts—he has resigned from the army, from motives of duty, and intends to study law, and devote himself in future to his father and Mother....

Septima Rutlege wrote from Chilhowee to her sister-in-law, Mary Helen, at Newport that September and expressed her grief over those lost on the *Pulaski*:

> ...I have loved our Dear Saint [Mary Helen's daughter, Maria Henrietta] from the earliest Age, but not until the last winter had I sufficiently appreciated the Exhalted Perfection of the Purity & sweetness of her character....The thought of the *sad chasmn* that the loss of this charming little Circle will make in your happiness...& the image of

my Lovely Niece is so associated with you all, that I cannot think of
any of you without a Pang....You still have many blessings left my
Dear Sister & many strong Ties to Life....This has in truth been a
melancholy summer to us all, & how often have I wish'd that we could
have passed it together....My children both near & at a distance have
all sympathized most truly in your affliction. They & Mr R. unite with
me in affectionate Remembrances to yourself, my Dear Brother & all
around you, & believe me my Dear Sister with much truth

> Y^r Sincerely attached
> Sister
> S: S: M: R: —

Septima wrote from Nashville in December to Mary Helen at Middleton Place reminiscing about the Christmas before:

....I most truly wish I could be near you all this Winter, but it would
have been out of our power to have returned so soon at all events, &
now that my Dear Arthur is restored to us Our Home no longer seems
Desolate....Our situation is a Beautiful one tho' & we ought to be
reconciled to the Exile from our Native Home as difficult as it is to
become so & endeavor not to repine for we have many Comforts, &
even Luxuries to enjoy....The approaching Season reminds me of the
happiness I enjoyed near you all last Winter, & I dare not dwell upon
the Sad Change in the Dear Circle that I love so much....may the next
year bring with it much comfort & many blessings....

By mid-October the travelers from Hampton had made their way to
Buncombe from their tour of the "Springs" to the north only to receive
word that Becky's brother, Pinckney Lowndes, had died. She wrote
Edward:

....My heart is like the nether millstone, I was ashamed of my insensi-
bility when poor Tom was taken—now my own dear brother is laid in
the cold grave, my favourite, my last; my playmate from infancy, he
whom I always looked up to more than a brother, whom I thought I
loved more than Sisters commonly loved their brothers, he is gone,
and I feel it not, I do not even weep....our two mothers are both griev-
ing over their children dear Edward, and it behooves us to devote ourselves to them, you to mine [in Charleston] and I to yours [traveling
with Becky], that they may each have cause to acknowledge that in us

two they have indeed two children—Harrie is well and enjoying herself very much—

Your's affte^b

R M Rutledge

Frederick wrote Edward concerning Becky and the family:

Buncombe County N C

October 25th 1838

My dear Edward

When our party from the Virginia Springs returned here every one of them so much improved by their excursion that I felt a regret that you were not at Murrrayville to welcome them....

He described the news of Pinckney Lowndes' death and then commented:

This is another instance, that most afflictions in this life befall us when least expected. I suppose you hear often from Becky—Harrie has got quite the spirit of the mountains & runs over the hills like a wild little mountaineer. She was all impatience to get to her "Dear Papa"—I hope she will escape the fate of an only child & never be a spoiled one. What a delight it will be to see her again after such a long & hard summer as we have had. My mother & sisters will soon be with you.

As the rest of the letter evidenced, Frederick had by this time been able to help his brother with plantation business without becoming oppressed by the magnitude of responsibility. Edward's willingness to remain in South Carolina kept Hampton from being neglected and gave both brothers a sense of accomplishment. They consulted one another and planned together for the most profitable ways in which to supervise their mother's property. Frederick reported to Edward:

....I rec^d a letter...from Council, in which he gave me a pretty good account of the Rice Crop at Harrietta & Waterhan, he mentions however that the carpenters' work was *very backward* owing to the sickness of Howe & Blacksmith Stephen (who usually works with the carpenters during the summer) now it appears to me that Pepper & Peter might be sent to Harrietta & be more usefully employed on the plantation than in town....The mill at Har^a ought to be put in as good order as

My Mother's own carpenters can repair it—I think that the interest of the plantation requires this, but I only wish it done if it meets her approbation—Do let me hear from you soon....The family here are all well but you will soon hear of us from those who have seen us....

Frederick added a note after closing which indicated a certain dependency on Hampton that still existed:

My wardrobe is both short and scant—if tailor Will is not otherwise engaged he can make two pair of trousers and one coat for me & send them by one of the Santee Coasters.

Photo—C. E. Staton, Jr.

Photo—C. E. Staton, Jr.

St. John in the Wilderness churchyard, Flat Rock, North Carolina:

Cross-shaped marker in foreground—Frederick Rutledge (1800–1884); Flat marker to back of cross—Henrietta Middleton Rutledge Rutledge (1807–1842).

The next few years brought great happiness to Frederick and his cherished family in Buncombe. A son born August 5, 1839, was named for Henrietta's father, Henry Middleton Rutledge. In May 1841 a daughter was named for Henrietta's sister and for Frederick—Emma Fredericka (she was called Minna). There was greater security and peace of mind than ever before with Hampton now well supervised, more productive, and, as always, a special place for family visits. In Buncombe County, North Carolina, Frederick, Henrietta, and their six children had found a home all their own. However Frederick's recent words to his brother would apply to his own circumstances all too soon—"most afflictions in this life befall us when least expected." On September 27, 1842, Henrietta died suddenly of a heart attack. She had not been ill so it was without warning that Frederick and the children were deprived of the one whose faith had kept all around her from dejection. Their wealthy neighbor and friend Mrs. Baring, who had shown particular interest in Henrietta, arranged for a lavish Victorian funeral at St. John in the Wilderness church. The children were dressed in black crepe which the older ones never forgot and the entire mountain community mourned with the family at the loss of their beloved Henrietta.

In Memory
of
Henrietta
wife of
Frederick Rutledge
In whom the rarest loveliness
and most attractive grace
combined with angelic benevolence
And genuine humility
To adorn a fine understanding
the finest principles of virtue
and unaffected Piety
Unblamed, unequalled in each Sphere of life,
The tenderest Daughter Sister Parent Wife
Died on the 27th of Sept. 1842
And in the 35th year of her age

The three youngest children (Alice, Henry, and Minna) were sent to live with Septima, Henrietta's mother in Nashville, while Frederick returned to Hampton and his mother Harriott, with Lize, Sally, and Edward.

Nine-month-old Elizabeth Pinckney Rutledge, the second and only other child besides Harrie ever born to Edward and Becky, died at Hampton that November of lung inflammation. Frederick's hope that his little niece Harrie not be reared alone would now become possible only because his own children would be part of the family at Hampton. Frederick never remarried although he lived until 1884. He sold Brookland to Edmund Molyneaux, British Consul to Savannah, Georgia, and thereafter traveled widely, never losing the memory of his pretty, dark-haired, cousin/bride from Tennessee.

Part V

THE COLONEL

Henry Middleton Rutledge (1839–1921)

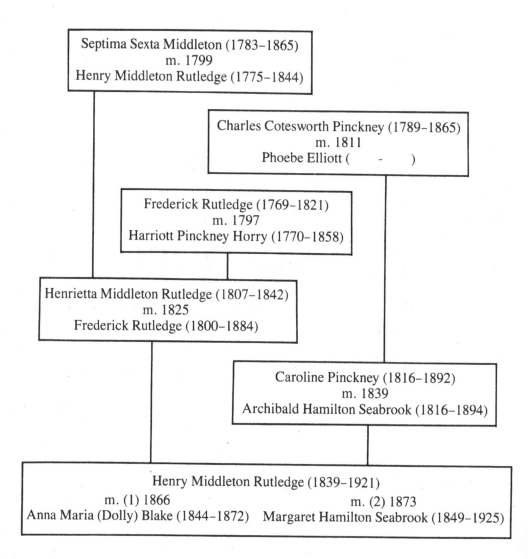

Septima Sexta Middleton (1783–1865)
m. 1799
Henry Middleton Rutledge (1775–1844)

Charles Cotesworth Pinckney (1789–1865)
m. 1811
Phoebe Elliott (-   )

Frederick Rutledge (1769–1821)
m. 1797
Harriott Pinckney Horry (1770–1858)

Henrietta Middleton Rutledge (1807–1842)
m. 1825
Frederick Rutledge (1800–1884)

Caroline Pinckney (1816–1892)
m. 1839
Archibald Hamilton Seabrook (1816–1894)

Henry Middleton Rutledge (1839–1921)
m. (1) 1866   m. (2) 1873
Anna Maria (Dolly) Blake (1844–1872)   Margaret Hamilton Seabrook (1849–1925)

Genealogy V—The Colonel
Henry Middleton Rutledge
(1839–1921)

96

Chapter 16

At the death of Henrietta Rutledge in 1842 her children Alice, Henry, and Minna had gone to live in Nashville. Henrietta's sister Mary, who was married to a prominent Nashville attorney, Francis Brinley Fogg, was to help her mother, Septima Rutledge, rear Henrietta's youngest children. Mary Fogg had three children of her own: Francis, Jr.; Septima; and Henry Middleton. Henrietta's children were brought into the family at Rose Hill and received every kind attention from their grandmother and aunt. It was at the Fogg home across from Christ Episcopal Church (the Rutledge and Fogg families had been the founders in 1830) that Major Henry Middleton Rutledge died at age sixty-eight, January 20, 1844. In her grief the education and welfare of Henrietta's children became a consolation for Septima. However in 1847 she became ill with arthritis, left her "sweet little charges" in school in Nashville "under the care of their Aunt Mary," and went to stay with her son Arthur at Chilhowee in Franklin County, Tennessee. At some point during this time, while Alice and Minna remained in Nashville, little Henry was taken to live at Hampton where he was able to spend more time with his father and the Rutledge family in Charleston. His sisters Sally and Lize were already at Hampton, as well as his brother Edward. Frederick Rutledge and his children still spent as much time as possible in Buncombe, with occasional travels to Philadelpha and the northern resorts to visit other family members who were on their summer circuits.

There is an interesting letter from seventy-year-old Sarah Rutledge (daughter of Edward the signer) written to her cousin Harriott Pinckney (daughter of Charles Cotesworth Pinckney). Cousin Sally had news of Frederick and young Henry who would be thirteen years old in three days. Harriott Pinckney was seventy-six when she received this letter and had not traveled that summer:

Philadelphia
2nd August 1852

My dear Harriott
....We had hardly seated ourselves at the tea table, before there was another ring at the bell, & to my surprise in walked Frederick, & dear little Henry. I can not tell you how much I was delighted, at seeing this

Darling Boy; & how truly I rejoiced to find him looking so healthy & well. He has a fine open countenance, & is certainly like my dear Father [Edward Rutledge, 1749–1800]; Mⁿ Drayton thinks he has his Mother's sweet smile, his voice too is very sweet; & if you were to see that Boy in a wig-wam you would say he was a gentleman's Son. He came again last evening, & his Father later; both were to leave Philadelphia today or tomorrow but neither the time not the rout [sic] were quite certain therefore if you receive this letter a day or two before they make their appearance, Cousin H Rutledge must not be uneasy, I sincerely hope she will perfectly have recovered before their arrival. Henry was very anxious to be at home on his Birthday; for his Grandmother's gratification as well as his own, I hope his wish may be realized. Give my love to her, & say I think we have the finest children in Carolina; & that I trust she is well enough to enjoy the return of her Pet....

Sarah Rutledge continued by telling her cousin she had had a long letter from a mutual friend who had thanked her for a package and her last two letters:

...the Grits, rice flour, & "last tho' not least," my invaluable book ....she has thought of me often; & has been procuring for me some receipts; that some of mine are *excellent,* & that I would be amused to hear the frequent applications to the Cook; that whenever any thing new appears on table, Lady Acland or herself send down to know whether it was made from Miss Rutledge's Book....

Believe me ever my Dear Harriott

Your affecᵗ friend __ S Rutledge

Harriott Pinckney and Sarah Rutledge shared the Pinckney mansion on East Bay above Market Street in Charleston. In 1847 Sarah had published a cookbook entitled *The Carolina Housewife or House and Home by a Lady of Charleston.* Her "receipts" were a marvelous collection of low-country dishes as well as those she had translated and saved from her travels in Europe. She made the directions understandable for the cook who might not be familiar with the equipment used by French or English servants. Her work included over 550 recipes with nearly 100 of them "in which rice or corn form a part of the ingredients." Her advice to the woman whose husband had thoughtlessly brought home unexpected company for dinner was: "A clean table-cloth and a smiling countenance." Sarah Rutledge died in 1855 at which time her niece

Mary Fogg wrote a lengthy tribute that outlined this outstanding woman's accomplishments:

IN MEMORIAM.

The late Miss Rutledge

of Charleston South Carolina.

Sarah Rutledge, only daughter of Governor Edward Rutledge, of South Carolina, one of the signers of the Declaration of American Independence, and sister of Henry Middleton Rutledge, of Nashville, Tennessee, departed this life on the 13th of April, after a very short illness, with a smile of holiest peace illuminating her benignant countenence, having nearly accomplished three-quarters of a century....A devout member of the Episcopal Church, she was one of its brightest ornaments, and one of its strongest pillars....Intrusted by her honorable father and sole remaining parent to the care of her maternal uncle, General Charles Cotesworth Pinckney, on his embassy as Minister Plenipotentiary to the Court of France, she was placed by him at the celebrated school of the distinguished biographer of Madame de Genlis, *Madam Campan*....here Miss Rutledge was intimately associated with daughters of the "ancien régime," and enjoyed numerous and brilliant advantages, never before or afterwards presented to a young American. Her polished manners were formed on the best models that European society could boast; but her principles were formed at home, in the school of true republican simplicity and lofty integrity, where courteousness is founded on sincerity and independence....the "Church Home," of which she was the happy founder, in her native city, for the support and education of destitute girls in the knowledge of the Bible and the purest principles of the Church, will send forth hundreds to bless *her* memory, whose mantle of protecting love was gently drawn over their defenceless heads, and whose voice implanted in their young hearts "seeds of glorious light," to bloom with sweetest fragrance through eternity. To the Sunday-schools in Charleston her time and talents were for many years, with unceasing zeal and energy, devoted....many a youthful mother and conscientious father now look back with delight to the persuasive eloquence with which she interested their tender hearts in the Saviour's dying love, and live to send through generations the precious fruits of her invaluable teaching....A numerous band of weeping orphans followed to the tomb the delicate casket which but lately held so rich and rare a treasure, and whence has fled that gentle, spotless spirit, to mingle with angels, for whose companionship she was so well prepared. The death of Miss Rutledge has left an "aching void" and a deep chasm in the large community, to which she was, in truth, a blessing and an honor, as well as to the purest principles of patriotism that distinguished her noble father, whose life and talents were devoted to the cause of freedom, and whose heart's best blood would, at any moment, gladly have been shed for his country. An extensive circle of friends in every part of this Union will hallow her memory in their affections: Zion mourns the loss of a favorite daughter....A fairy form of exceeding delicacy, and a joyous smile of benignity and peace were hers, with that true index of a lofty intellect, a large, well-opened, dark-gray eye, that sparkled with the light of the soul, and lost none of its brilliancy until it rested on the glories of heaven.

M. R. F.

Nashville, Tenn., June 4, 1855.

By this time Mary Fogg's two oldest children and Henrietta's Alice had died and were buried near their grandfather in the Nashville City Cemetery. Of the once large group of children in Nashville, only Minna and her cousin, Henry Middleton Rutledge Fogg, were left to cheer Septima and Mary and Francis Fogg. For this reason, Septima's son Henry Adolphus, his wife Caroline Bell, and their daughters Emma and Septima (called Seppie) left Alabama and moved to Nashville, staying at Rose Hill during the first few years of the 1850s. During that time word reached the Tennessee Rutledge family that Emma Blake had died at The Meadows in North Carolina. Mary Fogg wrote a memorial for Emma who was buried with their sister Henrietta in Flat Rock:

OBITUARY ON MRS. EMMA P. BLAKE

DEPARTED THIS LIFE, on the 21st of April, after a long, painful, and distressing illness...**EMMA,** wife of **Daniel Blake,** of Charleston, South Carolina, daughter of **Henry Middleton Rutledge,** of Nashville, Tennessee, and granddaughter of the Hon. **Edward Rutledge** and **Arthur Middleton,** signers of the Declaration of Independence.

Seldom has Death's icy shaft pierced a heart so noble, pure, and tender....Long years of suffering could not shake her fortitude, impair her faith, or diminish her energy....Intellectual in countenance, stately in height, and majestic in form....Her conversational talents were very remarkable, even to eloquence; her wit playful and sparkling, and

Emma Middleton Rutledge Blake (1812–1853). Detail of portrait thought to be painted c. 1841–1842 by Samuel Osgood.

her manners highly polished....Her's were indeed the children of *Prayer* and of the *"Church,"* of which she was a devout communicant-...this *devoted* mother [did]...expound to them "the word of God," ....she was her husband's councellor, friend and unfailling support ....As a *Sister,* she was the personification of *all* that is *tender* and *true*....volumes could not express the ardent devotion and overflowing gratitude that filled her soul for those venerated parents (to whose unceasing care she owed so much)....It remains but for her weeping family humbly to bow at the foot of the Cross, and say

"Thy will be done—
Hallelujah! hallelujah; praise the Lord!"
And then **PREPARE TO MEET HER.**

M.F___ .

Charleston—Printed by A.E. Miller

In 1856 Daniel Blake married again. He and his second wife, Helen Craig of New York, lived at The Meadows and reared five of the eight children who have been born to Emma, along with their own three. Septima Rutledge was now a widow with a daughter and two sons left of her eight children. By the close of 1853 her son Henry Adolphus left Rose Hill and settled his family in Marion County, Tennessee, at a plantation he named Woodlands. Now Mary Fogg was the one to help her mother in Nashville as Septima's youngest son Arthur had married Eliza "Light" Underwood of Bowling Green, Kentucky, and they continued to make Chilhowee a permanent home. In 1852 Eliza "Light's" stepmother,

Elizabeth Cox Underwood, visited Chilhowee to help with the birth of their first child. Writing to "Light's" father, Senator Joseph Rogers Underwood, just nine days before his granddaughter was born (Elizabeth Underwood Rutledge, b. August 29, 1852), she described her trip and the magnificent Rutledge estate:

> "Chilhowee", Coffee Cty. Tenn
>
> Friday August 20th 52

My dearest Husband

I have been domesticated here some days, enjoying myself very much. This day a week ago I left Bowling at sunrise in a hack, accompanied by Rogers and little Edith and a servant woman....I...stayed the night at the Tyree Springs, a distance of some 40 odd miles from B. Green, reaching it at sundown....The next morning I left for Nashville, where I arrived at dinner time....That evening after tea, I was visited by Judge Brown, M: & M: F. Fogg, V.K. Stevenson, and D: Martin. I remained in the City the next day....On the next morning (Monday) about 7 o'clock A.M., Eugene started with us on the cars which took us to Deckard's (85 miles) in 4 hours, there we found the stage ready which carried us 8¹/₂ miles to Hawkerville, where we found M: Rutledge awaiting us with a conveyance to take us across the country to this place, distant 3 miles thus making about 96 miles in all from Nashville to "Chilhowee" made in the interval between 7 in the morning & 1 o'clock P.M. So much for railroads.

This is one of the most picturesque spots I ever saw, and the air and water are pure and delightful. Numerous springs are on the plantation, which comprises at this one point a body of 5 or 6000 acres of land, 4 or 500 being under cultivation. M: Rutledge may sit on his portico and say "I am monarch of all I survey." The landscape is beautiful in the extreme. We are just at the beginning of the mountain ridge and our view looks over the gentle hill slope spotted with noble oaks, just in front of the windows to the valley beneath, through which runs the Elk River, not more than a hundred or two yards from the house. This is a fine trout stream and affords many a nice breakfast & dinner. M: R & Eugene being our anglers. In the valley beneath us, & just enough hid to add to the beauty, are the grist & saw mills, blacksmith's shop etc, the hum of the machinery, coming from the little distance with a softened and musical effect. Beyond this still, high mountains bound the range of vision almost on every side, with glimpses of green valleys at intervals and I assure you the "tout ensemble" is charming. A storm came up yesterday afternoon and gave me an opportunity of witnessing nature in one of her sublimest moods. It was really magnificent. It was raining sometime on the more distant hills before it reached us & it was curious to watch the clouds swooping down like huge eagles with outstretched wings, and hovering over the mountain tops, until a hazy atmosphere gradually enveloped all, and our range of vision was limited to the valley immediately at our feet. Eugene and I never tired with watching the shifting lights and shadows of the scene....

I have been luxuriating on watermelons, apples, peaches & pears, to say nothing of the draughts of delicious water which is nectar compared with its counterfeit in Bowling Green. The children are delighted. Little Rogers caught a fish all by himself on yesterday....

There are near a hundred negroes here of all ages. A little *shirt tail* regiment follows Rogers up & down the hills to the sound of his drum. An old woman (Delia) is still living, aged 95. She has lived with Edward Rutledge, the Signer, and remembers the revolutionary scenes in the South....She has her intellect perfectly & sews her own clothing. To be complimentary I suppose in return for my visits, she tells me "you look good too much."...

Eliza is...not so much of an invalid as I expected to find her....I should not be surprised if *the event* is delayed for some two or three weeks yet, or perhaps longer....Letters put in the office at Hawkerville (a little place on the edge of M: R's property, consisting of a store, blacksmith's shop & one, or two other little buildings only,) are sent across the country to Winchester, & fail to reach their destination under a very long time. The practice of this family & their Nashville relatives, is to put stamps on their letters & then send them by the hands of M: Sands the Railroad conductor and an accomodating person. This course loses nothing to Uncle Sam, & contributes much to the comfort of all concerned....

Most devotedly your
E.C.U.

Septima Rutledge and her granddaughter Minna often visited Chilhowee, Woodlands, and Middleton Place, where on occasion they would meet Frederick with the other children for family reunions. There were still many ties to Buncombe County, North Carolina, to the Blakes at The Meadows, and to Minna's own family at Hampton. On March 20, 1851, eighteen-year-old Harrie (daughter of Edward and Becky

Rutledge) married St. Julian Ravenel in Charleston. Weddings were the happiest times for gatherings of the Rutledge clan and excuse enough for a trip to South Carolina.

There was not a great deal of correspondence concerning Hampton during the 1850s but there seems to be evidence of declining productivity for the great rice plantations. For the United States, territorial expansion was a national policy and the questionable institution of slavery remained the dominant issue.

Chapter 17

Hampton Plantation remained the property of Harriott Rutledge until her death in 1858. She was buried in St. Michael's churchyard in Charleston with the following words to mark her grave:

Sacred
to the Memory
of
HARRIOTT PINCKNEY RUTLEDGE
Relict of
FREDERICK RUTLEDGE
Died October 13, 1858
"The Memory of the Just
Smells sweet and blossoms in the dust."

Within two years Edward Cotesworth Rutledge, the next legal owner of Hampton, was dead leaving the plantation properties to his brother Frederick. Harrietta had been sold in 1858 to Stephen D. Doar for $25,000. The next year Robertson, Blacklock and Company made the following factor's reports to Robert F.W. Allston:

Charleston Jany 13 1859

Dear Sir

....We broke down on the Sale of Mrs. Rutledge's Plantations on Santee to day, no bid or offer for those on the North River. Harrietta on the South River was sold to S.D. Doar for $25,000. There are some 60 negroes on same to be sold, can we do anything with you? at anything at or over $600 for them. They will be sold to pay debt is the worst of it and money is the strong component part! Still as they have to be sold, we must do the best we can for the Heirs, not losing sight of the future welfare of the people, and our desire to get them a good owner. But a large portion of cash is indispensable....

Charleston Jany 18 1859

Dear Sir

We received your favor of 17th. J B Allston has bought the Rutledge Negroes at $575 round. He will use the $10,000 paid in by Doar on his

105

purchase of Harrietta. Please send us the amount of cash for T P Alston's negroes $1500, if perfectly convenient and agreeable, if not however we will pay here only as you said you could send us a check, pray do whichever is most convenient. We can settle the difference on cost of Papers, etc at any time....

The following letter from Joseph Blyth Allston to Robert F.W. Allston confirms the factor's reports:

Charleston Jan 18th 1859

My Dear Uncle

I purchased the Harrietta gang of negroes to day at $575 round being $35,075 in all. Doar had previously offered $550 round. It is more than I should pay but the winter is passing with little prospect of their selling for less and the Waverly mill would perhaps be benefitted more by an increase of hands this winter than at any future time. The terms are 3000 cash balance within 7 years. I shall go up on the Steamer on Thursday receive the negroes at Harrietta and thence to Waverly. Frederick Rutledge had bought the driver which is a great drawback. There are 61....

Frederick retained ownership of Hampton until April 28, 1861, when he sold it to his twenty-one-year-old son, Henry Middleton Rutledge, for "Love and Affection." It had been almost twenty years since Henrietta's death; their only other son, Edward, had died in 1856 at age twenty and was buried at St. John in the Wilderness near his mother. His gravestone tells of his death:

Sacred to the Memory of
Edward Rutledge
who was born April 12, 1836
and died Aug. 5, 1856
Worthy of his ancestry, devoted
to his duties, uniting in a high
degree firmness of purpose with
mild and conciliating manners,
cultivated in mind and pure
in morals. He gave every promise
of an useful and happy future
when a severe and lingering
sickness, endured with uncomp-
laining meekness, took him
from his friends and family
to live in their memory
and with the Blessed forever

Photo—C. E. Staton, Jr.
Courtesy—Owners, Mr. & Mrs. Alexander Schenck, Flat Rock, North Carolina

The "Rutledge Cottage," Flat Rock, North Carolina.

Following Edward's death Frederick purchased a cottage in Flat Rock, North Carolina, from Dr. Mitchell King, son of Judge Mitchell King, one of Flat Rock's original developers. Dr. King had built this small dwelling and lived in it while work was being done on Glenroy (now Kenmure), which was long considered the most beautiful estate in the area. When construction of Glenroy was completed Dr. King's slaves placed the smaller edifice on great logs and moved it with teams of oxen to its present location about one-fourth of a mile from Glenroy. In 1857 Frederick's daughters, Lize and Sally, settled there dividing their time between Flat Rock and Hampton. This would give them, their father, and others of the family a Carolina mountain home for summer visits. This beautiful white structure become known as the "Rutledge cottage" and was a fine complement to the plantation at Hampton. The following decade would bring war and with it would come changes in economic stability but not in courage for those connected with Hampton.

President James Buchanan's State of the Union address in December 1860 presaged the conflict ahead:

> ....The different sections of the Union are now arrayed against each other, and the time has arrived, so much dreaded by the Father of his Country, when hostile geographical parties have been formed.

That November the South Carolina legislature called for a special convention to meet at Columbia on December 17 to discuss secession. On December 20 an ordinance passed by a unanimous vote to dissolve the union between South Carolina and the rest of the United States. The convention then demanded the return of Fort Sumter to South Carolina's authority. By December 30 South Carolina had seized the federal arsenal in Charleston completing the occupation of Charleston Harbor with the exception of Fort Sumter which was not surrendered. From January 1861 until June of that year ten slave states followed South Carolina's path of secession. Southern congressmen, politicians, and military personnel soon left the North to return home. A convention of the Confederate States of America gathered on February 4 in Montgomery, Alabama, and five days later elected Jefferson Davis of Mississippi provisional president. Abraham Lincoln was inaugurated as sixteenth president of the United States on March 4, the Confederate convention in Montgomery authorized the organization of an army on March 9, and at 4:30 A.M., April 12, southern General Beauregard ordered guns fired on the Federal troops at Fort Sumter forcing the Fort to surrender by 2:30 P.M., April 13. This action marked the beginning of the War Between the States.

Eliza Lucille Haskell Lee (1836–1905), described her "Reminiscences of Troublous Times, and God's Special Providences" in an unpublished manuscript:

> On an evening in December, 1860, whilst seated around the tea table at a farm, about two miles from Charleston, our family circle was much startled by the boom of cannon; two reports only, but sufficient to arouse our fears to the highest pitch. In silent wonderment we gazed at each other, as if asking an explanation. The unusual hour, the condition of the affairs of the country at the time, made us naturally tremble with an undefined dread of what was to come. We retired with gloomy forebodings to await the revelations of the coming morning, at which time the news reached us that Maj. Anderson had spiked the guns at Fort Moultrie, and taken possession of Sumter.

This act surprised and aroused the indignation of the people. Then came the summons "To Arms!", and our husbands, sons, and brothers, left their homes to obey the call of duty.

Our hearts grew faint then, so little we dreamed of the real terrors of war, yet to be experienced. We felt forlorn and forsaken, but at the same time the true "rebel" spirit and resolution burned in our hearts, and we were ready to do and suffer all that was in weak woman's power.

We moved into the City, and remained there during the winter of 1861, and in April, passed through our first trial of suspense and distress. Our batteries attacked Ft. Sumter, and during the attack we were cut off from communication with our men; exaggerated rumors of the number of lives lost, spread through the town, until the suspense seemed too great to bear. The truth at last brought joy and gratitude, for not one had perished. After two days struggle, Maj. Anderson surrendered.

The fact of our firing upon the "Flag" inflamed the entire North, and the war began in earnest.

The remainder of the summer and following winter, our lives, though filled with anxieties, were, outwardly, uneventful.

James Smith Middleton, a descendant of Arthur Middleton, wrote of his family situation as war began in Charleston:

....About this time, my father and his brother, Walter, decided to leave Charleston and become rice planters. They purchased a plantation on North Santee River, know as "Daisy Bank" and supplied it with the necessary equipment of negro slaves, etc. The family was moved to Daisy Bank about 1860, as nearly as I can calculate. I was born, in Charleston, during May 1856; and was, therefore too young, at that time, to have any definite recollection of the discussions which went on in regard to the approaching Civil War. My first real memory of anything of this kind was the gathering together of the planters who were summering on South Island. I later realized that this was for the purpose of cavalry drill, in preparation for joining the Confederate Army. This happened in the summer of 1861....

On May 20, North Carolina became the eleventh state to vote for secession and shortly thereafter ten companies of western Carolina mountain men were assembled at Camp Patton in Asheville, North Carolina, to organize the Twenty-fifth Regiment. Company H was commanded by Captain Frederick Rutledge Blake, twenty-three-year-old son of Emma

Photo—R. Alan Powell
Courtesy—Middleton Place Foundation,
Charleston, South Carolina.

Captain Arthur Middleton Rutledge
(1817–1876)—Commanding officer of
Rutledge's Battery, First Tennessee
Artillery, C.S.A.

and Daniel. Henry Middleton Rutledge, now twenty-two years old and the legal owner of Hampton Plantation, realizing war had begun, joined his cousin's regiment rather than return to South Carolina. That same summer their Nashville cousin, Henry Middleton Rutledge Fogg, was mustered into Rutledge's Battery: Company A, First Tennessee Artillery, commanded by their uncle, Arthur Middleton Rutledge. In September the Twenty-fifth North Carolina headed east while their Tennessee cousins moved into Kentucky as part of Brigadier General Felix K. Zollicoffer's forces at Cumberland Ford. On December 31, 1861, the artillery at Beech Grove, Kentucky, consisted of McClung's and Rutledge's batteries with fourteen guns. On January 19, 1862, at the Battle of Fishing Creek, General Zollicoffer was killed as was his aide-de-camp, Henry Fogg, leaving Major Arthur Middleton Rutledge distraught at the death of his commanding general and his own nephew. Henry Fogg's will mentioned Henry Rutledge's sisters Lize and Minna saying that Minna, who had been reared with him in Nashville, was "like my own sister."

In March 1862 twenty-two-year-old Henry Middleton Rutledge was elevated to the rank of colonel making him the youngest to hold that position in the Confederate army. Colonel Rutledge was a popular commanding officer leading his men in action under General Robert E. Lee at Seven Pines (Fair Oaks, Virginia), Petersburg, and Fort Steadman with the engagement at Antietam Creek near Sharpsburg, Maryland,

Courtesy—South Carolina State Parks, Recreation, and Tourism, Columbia, South Carolina.

Hampton Plantation—Legend of the South Santee.

One of America's stately homes, Hampton Plantation in the Carolina low country, was built during colonial times and inhabited continuously by the generations that preceded its final owner, Archibald Rutledge. In 1971 Dr. Rutledge sold Hampton for development as the focal point of a South Carolina state park assuring future preservation for the ancestral mansion he immortalized in **Home by the River.**

General Charles Cotesworth Pinckney (1746–1825), son of Charles and Eliza Lucas Pinckney.

Miniature by John Trumbull.
Photo—Silvia Sullivan
Courtesy—Estate of Edward R. Pinckney

General Thomas Pinckney (1750–1828), son of Charles and Eliza Lucas Pinckney.

Miniature by John Trumbull.
Photo—Silvia Sullivan
Courtesy—Estate of Edward R. Pinckney

Henry Middleton Rutledge
(1775–1844), son of Edward
Rutledge, South Carolina signer of
the Declaration of Independence.

Septima Sexta Middleton Rutledge
(1783–1865), seventh child, sixth
daughter of Arthur Middleton,
South Carolina signer of the Declaration of Independence.

Aerial view of Middleton Place House and Gardens, a Registered National
Historic Landmark on the Ashley River near Charleston, South Carolina.

Doctor Archibald Hamilton Rutledge (1883–1973)
Poet Laureate of South
Carolina.

Portrait by Alfred Jonniaux
Photo—Silvia Sullivan
Courtesy—House of Representatives, Columbia, South Carolina.

being the most costly of the Virginia and Maryland campaigns. Following Antietam, as Colonel Rutledge recrossed the Potomac under attack, he fell from his horse in mid-stream. Weakened by a wound and the onset of typhoid fever, he would have been lost save for the courage of Peter Williamson, his body servant from Hampton. Peter, who had safely reached the Virginia shore, returned under deadly fire to rescue the Colonel.

The many stories told of those long years of deprivation, fighting, and death give emphasis to the humility and gentleness which characterized the master of Hampton Plantation known as the "youngest colonel."

Chapter 18

The War Between the States altered the lives and fortunes of families, of cities, and of an entire nation, particularly the southern states. In South Carolina, Hampton Plantation escaped burning—Middleton Place did not. In Tennessee, Nashville was occupied from February 25, 1862 until the close of the War, during which time Lize Rutledge was with her grandmother and unable to return to Flat Rock. Rose Hill, Chilhowee, and Woodlands were damaged at the hands of the Federals. In Alabama, Seppie Rutledge (daughter of Henry Adolphus) married General John H. Forney in February 1863 and traveled with him to Vicksburg, Mississippi, only to witness the Confederate downfall and surrender, leaving her no choice but to return to Alabama.

By the close of 1865 many brave soldiers had been buried alongside those who had died while waiting for the brutal war's end. Major Arthur Middleton Rutledge returned to learn of the deaths of his wife "Light" (May 2, 1865) and his mother Septima (June 12, 1865).

Charleston is described by Harriott Horry Rutledge Ravenel (Edward and Becky's daughter Harrie) in her volume, *Charleston: The Place and the People,* which she completed in June 1906. The last chapter, "Confederate Charleston. The End" begins:

> In order to finish the story of Charleston, some mention of the war in which her old life ended must be made, briefly as possible....

She tells that the only supply that was plentiful was the manpower for the army—the arsenals were soon depleted and every woman worked to furnish uniforms:

> ....Ladies sat day by day among their maids, sewing shirts and trousers for the soldiers. The plantation tailors were brought out to help make the jean coats; knapsacks were fashioned of every conceivable thing, and people knitted as they breathed.

Plantations were kept alive by the very young and the very old servants who were left to guard what was their masters' security as well as their own. By 1864 only a few squares in Charleston bustled with activity beyond which "everything was overgrown with rank, untrimmed vege-

tation....The gardens looked as if Sleeping Beauty might be within
....The houses were indescribable....The streets looked as if piled with
diamonds, the glass lay shivered so thick on the ground....With the fall
of the city and the Confederacy went out the old life of Charleston...."
There seemed no end to the despair and yet the word "reconstruction"
soon characterized the South and its valiant attempts at recovery and
survival in the face of defeat.

Following Colonel Rutledge's return to Flat Rock, he married Anna
Marie Blake (called Dolly) who was a relative of his Blake cousins. To-
gether they journeyed to Hampton where a faithful remnant of the
Rutledge slaves had made every effort to maintain the property. A major
portion of each year was spent in Flat Rock with Frederick, Sally, and
Lize as well as with Dolly's family in Fletcher (by then Henderson
County, North Carolina). It was there in Henderson County that a son,
Frederick, was born to Henry and Dolly in February 1867. In 1870
Henry Rutledge built a log dwelling in McClellanville, less than a day's
ride from Hampton. This coastal village had emerged in the 1850s on
land belonging to A.J. McClellan with the earliest residents (planters
escaping malaria) being the Rutledge, Pinckney, Doar, and Manigault
families. Henry and Dolly Rutledge called their home in this tiny fishing

Photo—Genon Hickerson Neblett

St. James Santee chapel at McClellanville, South Carolina, used by summer
residents from the great Santee rice plantations.

village, the "Summer Place." Their pattern was to leave the plantation in early spring, go to McClellanville for a month, and then journey to Flat Rock. Time began to lessen the strain that war had caused, but Colonel Rutledge and his mountain-bride had only six short years together, for his precious "Miss Dolly" died February 21, 1872. It is known that the death of their infant daughter occurred during that same time so it is believed that complications of childbirth caused a stroke which took Dolly's life.

There is only one account of Dolly's death and it is not found in family records, diaries, letters, or newspapers of the period. This amazing, detailed portrayal is given today by Hampton's native guardian angel, Sue Alston. Born to Sarah and Lewis Colleton, Sue is the widow of Prince Alston, son of Martha and Will Alston, and although her exact age is unknown this direct descendant of Rutledge slaves is able, year after year, to give a clear picture of the day Dolly Rutledge died. In a recent interview, speaking in rich tones of patois Gullah, Sue repeated her story:

> My great-grandmother she be named Lydia Colleton—she come with Miss Dolly after she get married to Henry Rutledge....My great-grandmother, Lydia, she be name Lydia—she was an Indian. She had all that old long hair.

> Nobody have told me what I telling you because if I told you all somebody else begin and it wasn't my begin I can't answer with nobody else.

> When Miss Dolly die she left that boy Fred settin' in the window. I was little girl with my great-grandmother. I was over four years old and there when Miss Dolly put Master Fred in the window and she fell on the floor...and when the out cry—when my grandmother run in the room and hear the tumblin' and Master Fred was whoopin' cryin' and when my grandmother run in the room I run right behind her holding—she take 'um knockin' me off the apron....I was holding her and she was goin in the room so fast and I couldn't go as fast as her, and Missis, I had, you see the chillun eat in pan then you know, the round pan—she done fixin' my breakfast—milk, egg, and bacon....I had me pan in me left hand and I grab old grandmother and I hold her. She had a time but I get in the room with her....Miss Dolly, she was on the floor.

> Master Fred....was sittin' in the window and had his feet was beatin' them again' the wall—He was callin' my grandmother to tell them that this woman was on the floor.

Photo—C. E. Staton, Jr.

Calvary Episcopal Church (established 1859) Fletcher, North Carolina.

Photo—C. E. Staton, Jr.

Part of the Blake section in Calvary Episcopal churchyard, Fletcher, North Carolina. Flat stone on the left—Anna Maria Rutledge, wife of Henry Middleton Rutledge and daughter of Walter Blake.

Sue tells how Dolly was taken to Fletcher, North Carolina, to be buried near others of the Blake family in the churchyard of Calvary Episcopal Church. It had been founded just prior to 1860 with the organizational meeting held at The Meadows hosted by Daniel Blake, his second wife Helen, and others of the community. According to Sue, just six months after Dolly's death her grief-stricken Cherokee Indian nursemaid Lydia was also dead.

Colonel Rutledge remarried within a few years. He and his second wife, Margaret Hamilton Seabrook, had six children: Caroline Phoebe (b. Hampton, 1876); Harriott Horry (b. Hampton, 1878); Thomas Pinckney (b. Hampton, 1879); Henry Middleton (b. McClellanville, 1882); Archibald Hamilton (b. McClellanville, 1883); and Mary Pinckney (b. Hampton, 1886).

Sue Alston tells about Hampton and her beloved "Miss Margaret."

> Miss Margaret teach me it's a good thing to keep your manners and principles....I think 'bout some the old jobs Missis til I have a cry ....the people...they raised plenty hogs, cows, chickens, raised rice, people come to the gate every Friday....I think some time and I cry, because I know if Hampton had open I would have more coffee, more nice slice of bread than enough....My job was noble....The pretty woods on the left going out. She [Margaret] had a pretty oak and go 'neath that oak and sit down and she called me everyday at 12 o'clock. I carry that comb and that brush and comb her hair....we used to play shinny ball too much....[Colonel and Mrs. Rutledge] they the people had my wedding...pay one dollar to the preacher...I had some *people* in Hampton....Hampton, no plantation like a Hampton. No spot of ground—you couldn't name no other spot that been here like Hampton....I never work for anybody else....Now if you do right and live a life that the Lord intend you to live you'll see Heaven....Yes Lord, in America you got to live right, Yes Lord.

The Rutledge children and servants alike learned their "manners and principles" from Margaret Rutledge and they observed first-hand a compassionate generosity in her husband the "Colonel."

The period of "reconstruction" brought with it a new era in plantation management compatible to that of small farms with produce raised to sustain the lives of those who lived there and the surplus sold to provide clothing and funds for education of the children. During this time Hampton's greatest assets were the business ability of Margaret Rutledge and the ingenuity of the Colonel. Margeret's role as mistress of Hampton now included what could have been the unduly demeaning task of raising chickens and tending a vegetable garden had she not also maintained a cultural environment worthy of her background. She carefully guarded

Margaret Hamilton Seabrook Rutledge (1849–1925).

Hampton's income with the increasing determination that their youngest son, Archibald, would be sent to college. Her dream became reality and Archibald referred to his mother's work with the baby chickens in a letter he wrote her while in school. He said, "I picture to myself your little incubator babies and the cares connected with their raising. It must seem almost like 'twenty years ago' to you when there were real babies rending the nether air with their wails and making a big house seem too small."

While his wife acted as overseer Henry Rutledge served for a time as a local postman and created an ironic source of revenue. This youngest colonel of the Confederacy made his plantation available as a veritable playground for those who so recently had been his enemies. All of Hampton lined the bank of Wambaw Creek to greet their "guests," the hunting parties of wealthy sportsmen from the North who eagerly paid for the privilege of enjoying Colonel Rutledge's lush marshes and pinelands once known as the French Santee. In addition to these resources, the industrious couple took in summer boarders at Flat Rock and somehow managed to pay the taxes on Hampton, still financing the much-hoped-for college education of their son Archibald. The prolific writings of this tall, sensitive young man, who was destined to become

South Carolina's first poet laureate, were the culmination of his parents' loving sacrifices and worthiest expectations blended with his own talent and reverence for the generations before him who had made Hampton Plantation their home.

In September 1886 an earthquake hit the Charleston area just as full recovery from war's destruction had seemed a possibility. Sue Alston remembers her grandmother standing in the yard at Hampton watching a boiling pot of cow peas. She said that when everything shook, her grandmother's husband Sabey started to run away and her grandmother shouted after him saying that if he ran away he "better never come back." Sue said Sabey didn't return and her grandmother married a good Waccamaw Island man.

A member of the Lucas family from The Wedge on the Santee River was in Charleston during the "great shake" and wrote her family c/o South Island, Georgetown, South Carolina:

Chas^{in}

Sept 2nd 1886

....You will see by papers that our dear old city is a wreck, but nothing but eyesight can convey its extent. The earthquake night before last at one sudden moment did the worst....We spent the night in the middle of the street & suffered from successive shocks up to 8:20 A.M. but have no further disastrous quake. From midday we had a renewal of shocks some fainter, some severe, up to twelve last night, followed by distinct yet distant rumblings till 4:30 A.M. Since then all has been still....No words can convey the shrieks...mingled with praying & shouting which rose above the roar. Everybody is in the street day & night—houseless families on mattresses eating breakfast, dinner & supper....We hope today to eat a warm dinner, as there was such exploding of lamps, & overturning of stoves that fires broke out on every hand....let us know whether you did escape & are all well....

This event extended the period of rugged survival and of rebuilding for Charleston. A poignant letter written by the Colonel's sister Sally, who became the third wife of the Reverend Charles Cotesworth Pinckney, painted a stark picture of the times. She was answering a query from F.W. Leach who was compiling data on the descendants of the signers by contacting their grandchildren.

From Mrs. C.C. Pinckney, Charleston, S.C.
Jan. 4th, 1887

F.W. Leach, Esq.,

Dear Sir:

I have filled the blanks you sent me and added such information as I could. Some of our family are indifferent to the preservation of family records; but during the late war nearly all the homes of its members were plundered and burnt and it is impossible for this generation to repair the loss. Since the war our branch of the family has been engaged in the state of the battle of life, called keeping the wolf from the door and have little leisure for hunting up on old records....

Yours truly,
S.H. Pinckney.

Miniature by Bounetheau.
Courtesy—Owner, Sarah Pinckney Ambler,
Pass Christian, Mississippi

Sarah Henrietta Rutledge Pinckney (1832–1906).

Part VI

THE POET

Archibald Hamilton Rutledge (1883–1973)

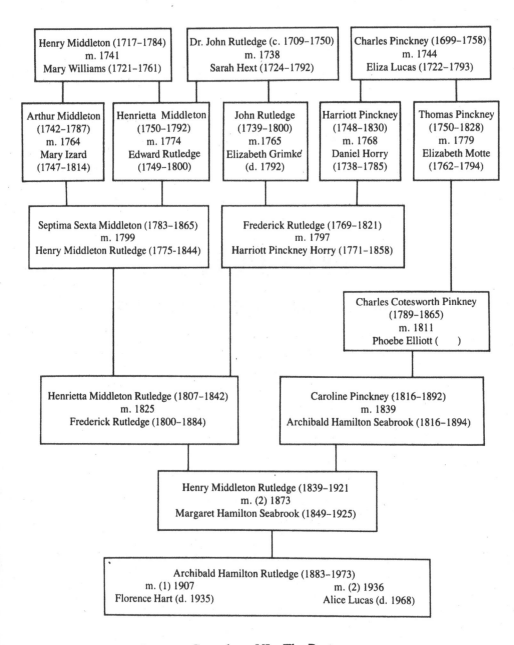

Henry Middleton (1717–1784)
m. 1741
Mary Williams (1721–1761)

Dr. John Rutledge (c. 1709–1750)
m. 1738
Sarah Hext (1724–1792)

Charles Pinckney (1699–1758)
m. 1744
Eliza Lucas (1722–1793)

Arthur Middleton
(1742–1787)
m. 1764
Mary Izard
(1747–1814)

Henrietta Middleton
(1750–1792)
m. 1774
Edward Rutledge
(1749–1800)

John Rutledge
(1739–1800)
m.1765
Elizabeth Grimké
(d. 1792)

Harriott Pinckney
(1748–1830)
m. 1768
Daniel Horry
(1738–1785)

Thomas Pinckney
(1750–1828)
m. 1779
Elizabeth Motte
(1762–1794)

Septima Sexta Middleton (1783–1865)
m. 1799
Henry Middleton Rutledge (1775-1844)

Frederick Rutledge (1769–1821)
m. 1797
Harriott Pinckney Horry (1771–1858)

Charles Cotesworth Pinkney
(1789–1865)
m. 1811
Phoebe Elliott (   )

Henrietta Middleton Rutledge (1807–1842)
m. 1825
Frederick Rutledge (1800–1884)

Caroline Pinckney (1816–1892)
m. 1839
Archibald Hamilton Seabrook (1816–1894)

Henry Middleton Rutledge (1839–1921)
m. (2) 1873
Margaret Hamilton Seabrook (1849–1925)

Archibald Hamilton Rutledge (1883–1973)
m. (1) 1907   m. (2) 1936
Florence Hart (d. 1935)   Alice Lucas (d. 1968)

Genealogy VI—The Poet
Archibald Hamilton Rutledge
(1883–1973)

122

Chapter 19

Archibald Hamilton Rutledge was born October 23, 1883 at the "Summer Place" in McClellanville just nine months before the death of his eighty-three-year-old grandfather, Frederick Rutledge. Young Archibald's abilities were obvious to his parents at a very early age and his mother was determined not only to teach him all she could but to secure a formal education for him no matter the sacrifice. He was sent to Miss Annie Ashburn Lucas at The Wedge, a neighboring plantation, for pre-school training followed by elementary boarding school in McClellanville.

From there he entered Porter Military Academy in Charleston, where he was salutatorian of his class in 1900, followed by graduation as valedictorian in 1904 from Union College in Schenectady, New York. While at Union College Archibald worked at odd jobs to supplement his scholarship and the money he received from home, and he also found time to edit a campus publication and write for other journals. Letters to his mother evidence his continued interest in literature and in composition, and his concern for the family at Hampton:

Union College
Schenectady, NY
Feb. 2nd '02

My dear Mama;

How I wish you could be here to see this snowstorm; it is one of the prettiest I have ever seen....Well! What will Papa do now? I can't imagine his not planting rice and I know the outlook must be gloomy for him...."We" formed a Southern Club....I hope it will live and show as much spirit as the club of '61, who raised the flag of secession...on our campus....

June 8th '02

....I am trying to get a little library tho' with my means it naturally progresses very slowly; do you think there are any books at Hampton that you could spare me;—just for a while? I would like poetry or something like Scott or Cooper better than anything else....

July 20th '03

....My little library is coming on slowly—I try to get books that have lived and will live; tho' of course I cannot always get what I want to— Hope Papa is well; and standing those long drives in hot weather is nothing to laugh about....

Nov. 22nd 1903

....You cannot imagine how much I enjoy the work and feel surer every day that I am not making a mistake in looking forward to it as my life's work. Yes, I have to write all the editorials and must edit every line of the other material....Have been getting on well with my verses of late—favorable criticisms from the exchanges & "the Winthrop Journal," a pretty good college monthly has quoted my "Music of the Pines":—I wrote eight pieces last night....

Courtesy—Eleanor Stevenson Rutledge, Jacksonville, Alabama

Archibald, Florence, and Archibald Rutledge, Jr. at home in Mercersburg, Pennsylvania.

After graduation Archibald worked for a short time as a newspaper reporter in Washington, D.C., before becoming a substitute teacher at Mercersburg Academy, Mercersburg, Pennsylvania. This "temporary" position lasted for thirty-four years, as with time he became head of the English department and part-time registrar. In 1907 he married Florence Louise Hart, a beautiful, creative writer from Washington who bore him three sons: Archibald Hamilton, Jr. (1908); Henry Middleton IV (1910); Irvine Hart (1912).

Archibald's parents were very proud of his accomplishments as his father expressed in April 1915:

> ...My Dear Boy I can well understand when you say you can get much our of your position & work besides your actual salary, your surroundings your daily contact with fine men, men of letters, & *caliber*. Yours is truly one of the noblest professions, finer & greater than the law. We had in our family Governors—lawyers & Dr·—Navy & Army men—planters farmers—clergymen bishops—but not a teacher, & a high toned instructor & educator such as my fine son is. Mores the pity....You are the most admired of the family—Education down here & anywhere is held in the highest esteem. Men of letters—Education & brains—who are looked up to, respected & admired....

In January 1921 the Colonel wrote Archibald that at Hampton the previous Sunday they had entertained thirty-three people from the Santee Club of Charleston, a hunting club. He referred to it as "Paul Seabrook's club." Paul Edmund Seabrook had married Archibald's sister Harriott at Hampton April 14, 1909. A description of that wedding written by Frederick Rutledge, son of Colonel Rutledge and his first wife Dolly, appeared many years later in a small volume of recollections, *Fair Fields of Memory*, privately published by his son, Frederick Reeves Rutledge.

An Old Plantation Wedding Is Recalled
By One Who Was There

Did you ever attend a genuine old-time plantation wedding? I have had that pleasure, but it was a long, long time ago. It was at my father's plantation home on South Santee River, known as Hampton. He raised large crops of rice, worth $1.50 a bushel, and the rich lands produced 50 to 60 bushels per acre. Hampton plantation comprised 2,500 to 3,000 acres mostly rice lands, though corn, cotton, and potatoes were also planted. It was not necessary to raise cattle, as game was plentiful—deer, wild turkey, duck, quail, woodcock, snipe and rabbits. No cost—you just had to hold your gun straight.

Well, one of the family decided to become a bride. She was charming, pretty, bright and the man who got her was surely lucky. The wedding was in the famous ballroom in which George Washington, LaFayette, Gen. Thomas Pinckney, and John Rutledge,

Chief Justice of U.S. Supreme Court, were entertained. In the front yard were saddle horses, horses and buggies, and an old ox hitched to a cart. Any old way, so long as you got to the wedding! The old colored women were there in their calico dresses and bandana handkerchiefs around their necks, and old men who wore the best they had—but they were welcome. There was handshaking and curtsying.

I went to the back door to see if guests from Georgetown were coming and saw what looked like a small steamboat making its way up Wambaw Creek, which was only about 75 yards from the house. On the deck I made out the Hazzard girls, young and most attractive, who later came to live in Asheville. I went back to the front yard, where two old women were crying. When I went up to them and asked what was the matter, they said—"Missie is leavin' and what are we goin' to do without her!" I told them not to cry—that I was sure she would come often to see the family. They grabbed each other's hands and said: "Thank the Lord! We hope she'll come when Wambaw rice is blossoming and Hampton roses are in bloom."

The Rev. Wilson K. (Bishop) Capers performed the ceremony, if memory serves me correctly. The carriage came up and bride and groom looked like they had been in a snowstorm. Rice! Rice! And several old shoes were in evidence that looked like they had come out of the ark.

The family gathered in the drawing room for midday dinner and if I told you all the things to be eaten your mouth would water. Then, one of the party suggested a deer hunt and there was not a dissenting vote. We mounted our horses and were off. One of the party killed a fine buck. As the sun was getting low we turned homeward. That was the end of a perfect day.

Half sister Harriot Horry Rutledge married a Seabrook of Savannah, Georgia.

Frederick Rutledge spent eighteen years of his life with his mother's sister and her second husband, Louisa Patience Blake [Heyward] and James Rose Rutledge in Flat Rock. Their one-hundred-acre estate, Dunroy, overlooked Sugar Loaf, Bear Wallow, and Bird Wing mountains and had been settled by the brother-in-law and sister of Mary Boykin Chestnut, author of *Diary from Dixie*. Following graduation from Virginia Military Institute, Frederick chose Asheville, North Carolina, as his home where in 1888 he began a fire insurance business that became the largest in North Carolina within fifteen years. However, holidays at Hampton provided contact with his father and half-brothers and sisters. The Thanksgiving and Christmas deer hunts there were the highlights of the year for all the Rutledge family as they gathered with their children to be near the Colonel and Margaret. A reminiscence of Christmas celebrations is provided by one of the Seabrook daughters, Harriott, who, along with her sister Margaret, retains vivid memories of festive visits with their grandparents:

....My earliest recollection of Hampton was of coming up the old Oak Ave. (not the one you see now) at dusk with Mother, my father and sister and seeing the lamps lit and the house aglow. We had driven from Savannah and were very tired. The wonderful experience of having so many relatives rush out to greet us and the marvelous smell of supper being cooked. We usually arrived the day before Christmas Eve. On

Courtesy—Eleanor Stevenson Rutledge, Jacksonville, Alabama

Colonel Henry Middleton Rutledge and his grandson, Archibald Rutledge, Jr.

the eve of Christmas we would go out with grandfather and one of the Negro men and pick out our Christmas Tree, which was always a Holly with lots of berries. This was taken into the Ball Room, put up, and decorated with cardboard stars that had pictures pasted on both sides and tinsel all around the edges. The real candles were placed on the bows and Grandfather would stand around with a long stick and wet cotton to put out any one that began to sputter. All of our stockings were hung around the Ball Room fireplace. There was Grandmother, Grandfather, Mother, Dad, my sister Margaret, Uncle Archie, Aunt Florence and their 3 boys, Aunt Mary, Aunt Caroline and me. Uncle Tom, Aunt Ethel and 3 daughters Ethel, Henrietta and Alice and their two sons. Tom and Hugh came early Christmas day. The gifts were the usual things but especially books. After the tree was lit the Negros would come in for their gifts and everyone sang spirituals and Christmas Carols. We had fire crackers that we would shoot; but we had to be sure to go away from the house to do that. The black people I remember particularly were Sue, Martha, Suzie, Ham, Prince and Missy. The food was typical Christmas fare—Turkey, Sweet Potatoes, Rice, Fruit Cake etc....

Of all his children Archibald remained special to the Colonel who was fond of calling him "Benjamin" just as the Old Testament patriarch Jacob had named his youngest son. During the Colonel's last few months his letters to Archibald exhibited their closeness:

....My Benjamin...your fine book *[Plantation Game Trails]* recd & I have finished six chapters & mama had to...insist on my writing to you....I intended writing anyhow, but she feared I'd never put down the book till long after bed time. I like your book very much & you write with such care & fluency & all your describing is so good—true, clear & to the point....I'm rejoicing at the prospect of Coin that is to come your way at last. You have worked hard & are entitled to every dollar you may receive....congratulate me—for the first time in five months, I eased myself into the Saddle today & am none the worse for it. My back now is the only trouble, somewhat stiff & painful at times but even that may wear off....I do so long to see the three—Mid & Irvine I know have developed greatly since I last saw them, Irvine must be a most lovely clever & attractive Child. We are well. Sister [Caroline] about runs the house. I can do but little, Mama is fairly well and devoted to her garden....

Hampton
3.14.21

Benjamin my Beloved—

I read your book everyday—I pick it up & read a chapter & it does me good...it is done in such a masterly way....Yesterday we all went in Caroline's car to Church in McC. [McClellanville]....I just long to see you—It does not appear to me that I am as happy as I should be ....You know *I* am *not* planting, Prince does it all or has it done....

Later that spring Archibald's father wrote:

....We are having summertime & the trees are bursting forth....wonderful Jassmine blow & the wild honeysuckle & cherokee rose vines overhanging the "Patch" will soon be a mass of lovely white (single roses)....I improve but do not stand *straight* as yet, but little pain in back when I do not over do it. You must try, not ever, to *stoop*—Try & stand erect always—it saves the day....

H M R

Photo—Charles Gay
Courtesy—South Caroliniana Library, Columbia, South Carolina
Colonel Henry Middleton Rutledge (1839–1921) and companion.

The Colonel died June 10, 1921, in McClellanville at the "Summer Place" and was taken to Flat Rock where he was buried the following Sunday in the Rutledge plot, St. John in the Wilderness churchyard. Along with the obituaries and eulogies were the letters of condolence. One poignant message was sent to the Colonel's oldest son Frederick then living in Asheville, North Carolina, from G.S. Fergason who had been eighteen years old when Henry Middleton Rutledge became his commanding officer in the Confederate army.

Waynesville N.C.
June 22nd 1921

My dear Friend!

    The first I learned of your Noble Fathers death was the article in the *Citizen*....Sunday morning...I some how thought of Col Rutledge and our first personal acquaintance—which was while our Regiment was at Grahamville S.C. in the winter of 1861....I was wondering if he was still living—Your Father—was a true man—a true and gallant Soldier—He was proud of his Regiment and loved his men—and they trusted and loved him. They would go where he said to go and follow him in the thickest of the fight—He had the splendid trait of character in war and peace which made the name of Rutledge in history of the Palmetto State synonymous with true greatness—Your Father was loved and respected to the outer circle of his acquaintance—He has left you the Rutledge name untarnished—the richest inheritance a Father can leave his children. I deeply sympathize with you and the family—I realize I have lost a true friend....

In less than four years Margaret Rutledge died at Fairfield, the Santee plantation which had belonged to her great-grandfather, Thomas Pinckney. She was also buried in Flat Rock at St. John in the Wilderness and her life was remembered by the women of her congregation, St. James Santee, with the following resolution:

    Entered into Life everlasting on the morning of February 23rd. 1925,

Margaret Hamilton Rutledge.

    She was our Leader and first President, unanimously elected when the Woman's Auxiliary was formed in this Parish January 1899. After twenty-one years of faithful, intelligent and enthusiastic leadership she resigned January 20th. 1920, but remained a loyal, helpful mem-

Photo—C. E. Staton, Jr.

Tombstone—Colonel Henry
Middleton Rutledge (1839–1921),
St. John in the Wilderness church-
yard, Flat Rock, North Carolina.

Photo—C. E. Staton, Jr.

Tombstone—Margaret Hamilton
Seabrook Rutledge (1849–1925),
St. John in the Wilderness church-
yard, Flat Rock, North Carolina.

ber for the rest of her life and always an inspiration and force in our
circle and community.

She led us in Church and Sunday School work, training the childish
minds and voices, and supplying music for the services of the Church
for many years. A cultured Christian woman, true and steadfast in
every relation of life has joined the Church Triumphant, and we pray
with full hearts to follow her good example and teaching.

Whereas it has pleased our Loving Father to take her to Himself, we
her sorrowing friends, co-workers and children in the Faith, resolve
that a blank page in our minute book be inscribed to her memory and
that a copy of this tribute be sent to her sorrowing children with our
loving sympathy.

Of all the tributes to Colonel and Mrs. Rutledge, the most moving
came from their son Archibald in his book, *My Colonel and his Lady,*
published in 1937. His words did not reiterate his parents' deeds or pos-
sessions but ably captured the "glory" in lives well spent, which was his
legacy.

Chapter 20

Following the deaths of Henry and Margaret Rutledge, Hampton was once again without an owner-in-residence. It was unoccupied except when Archibald spent holidays and vacations there along with his brother Tom, their sisters Caroline, Harriott [Seabrook], Mary [Stroman], and all the grandchildren. Caroline Rutledge, eventual owner of Fairfield Plantation, was the oldest, never married, and was an authority on Negro spirituals. Of the six children born to the "Colonel and Miss Margaret" only his namesake, Henry Middleton Rutledge III (known as Hugh), did not live to reach adult age. Hugh was born the year before Archibald and the two were close companions until eleven-year-old Hugh was killed by a train in September 1893. Since he survived the accident while playing, Archibald felt the trauma of his brother's death keenly, and that is often reflected in his writing. Archibald and Hugh had the most loyal of playmates in Prince Alston so that at Hugh's death "Arch" and Prince became inseparable. While Archibald was away at school he was always anxious to return to Hampton, to the hunt, and to Prince. As the Colonel aged and became unable to farm, Prince, Sue, their sons Prince, Will, Samuel, and their other children all did what was necessary for the upkeep of Hampton. Their dedication endeared them to the five Rutledge heirs, and the well-being of Prince Alston and his family came to mean that the homeplace was secure.

Following Christmas holidays of 1927 Archibald, Florence, and their sons, Arch, Jr., Mid, and Irv, were leaving Hampton for Pennsylvania when Prince asked Archibald to get out of the car for a last goodbye saying he just wanted to see Archibald one more time. Prince was evidently heeding a premonition, for by the next August he was dead. Archibald's sister Mary, who lived nearby, wrote her brother describing the circumstances of their loss and reassuring him that Sue would be well-cared-for.

Thursday August 2nd [1928]

Dearest Beloved—

The worst has happened, and we lost Our Prince at 4 o'clock this morning. I was a little more satisfied about him yesterday for a while but later I saw that there could not be much hope held out for him, although I sent you a card, endeavoring to make it as brave as I could—

132

Courtesy—Alston family, Hampton Plantation

Alston family at Hampton (c. 1925)—left to right: Will Alston, Martha Alston, Prince Alston, Sue Alston, and young Will Alston.

I was going up early this morning and was going out of the village when the message was given me. Of course I went right on up, and found every one very quiet. His two daughters had come from Charleston since Monday morning—but young Prince was at camp— Some one went for him this morning—Prince looked very much at rest—and all suffering, had gone from his face. Sue had one hard weep when I was there, but she soon was quiet again. Martha was a pitiful picture...making no out cry. I brought young Lewis back with me, & ordered the casket....They will sit up to night at the church, and bury him tomorrow morning at Hampton—It seems that Prince has not been feeling well, for some time, but when he was taken sick Sat. before the last...the case was desperate from the beginning; poisoning had set in, in the upper bowel, & intestine, and his entire system was congested— his throat was swollen on one side, & swallowing was extremely diffi-cult....I did all I could to save him; but he has left us, and I feel all at Sea and bewildered, and broken hearted. He was not in much pain at any time; his *extreme* weakened state caused him to lapse into periods of unconciousness; and often delirium. His Preacher was up on Tuesday—& said the Lord's Prayer, and the *Belief,* in *perfect* English, and sang two verses very softly, "God's Arms Shall Cover You"—and then talked to Prince a short while, giving him strength and courage and faith—It was not too much for his strength, but I would not have permitted more. Of course I am going up in the morning and will take the minister. I told Sue I would write you at once, and she said she wanted you to find some man to put in Prince's place, to over see the repair on piazza, cutting up of walnut tree, & riding the woods. She said the deer were very plentiful in the pasture, around witch pond, and even around the house; over the little bank. You don't know how keenly it grieves me to have to write you of this great loss to you, to Hampton, and to all who were associated with him....Prince belonged to three "Lodges," and a "Society"—so financially Sue is "well fixed"—For I *know* for a *fact,* that the "Lodges" take care of *all* funeral expenses, and in a few weeks, the widow receives from $250.00 to $300.00 from each one of them—I know so many cases where such is true—the money is good. So you must not worry on that score—for all who are members of these mysterious lodges testify that the money never fails to come....I can't write more this time.

> Devotedly yours
>
> Mary S.

With Prince gone Archibald, Tom, and their sisters had to be more concerned than ever with the upkeep of Hampton. Prince's family stayed in touch with Archibald and wrote him whenever there was word that Archibald might not be well. Two almost identical letters were written to Archibald in 1932 by Will and "Sam'l" Alston:

> Febry 11 1932
> Santee S.C.

> dear dos [boss] i rede your letter anb[d] was glab[d] to herb[d] from you i am so sory...when i herb[d] that you ar[are] not well....i think about the time we hab[d] Chrismas night that was a finb[fine] time at hampton....Will

> Febry 11 1932
> Santee S.C.

> dear doss[boss] i got you letter and was glab[d] to herb[d] from you and to now[know] that you ar[are] well....we saw some turky on the water....Saml Alston

Archibald continued his teaching at Mercersburg Academy and planned undergraduate training for all three of his sons, still yearning to return to Hampton, the subject of almost all his poems, articles, and books. By 1934, his prolific talent, his skill with words, and his love for South Carolina had gained him a long overdue and much deserved distinction.

STATE OF SOUTH CAROLINA
Office Of The Governor
Columbia

March second,
1 9 3 4

Hon. Archibald Rutledge,
Mercersburg, Pa.

My dear Mr. Rutledge:

Governor Blackwood requests me to inform you that he has today, in recognition of your contribution to South Carolina literature, appointed you Poet Laureate of South Carolina.

This appointment is made by virtue of authority vested in the Governor in a Joint Resolution passed by the General Assembly at its present session, which reads as follows:

"Be It Resolved by the General Assembly of the State of South Carolina: That the Governor of this State be, and he is hereby authorized and empowered to name and appoint some outstanding and distinguished man of letters as poet-laureate for the State of South Carolina."

Formal notice of your appointment has been forwarded to the Office of the Secretary of State and a commission will be mailed to you from that Office.

Yours very truly,
Chas. H. Gerald
Secretary to the Governor.

However, the glow surrounding this honor could not brighten the empty spots in Archibald's heart for his parents, Hugh, and Prince, nor could the recognition remove the loss he felt when his wife died suddenly of a stroke while they were visiting Charleston in 1935. There would have to be a change and some security for Hampton before South Carolina's first poet laureate could find that "peace in the heart" that he wrote about so often.

He arranged priorities: the completion of his sons' educations; the

Courtesy—Eleanor Stevenson Rutledge, Jacksonville, Alabama

Florence Hart Rutledge and Archibald Rutledge, Jr.

early retirement from Mercersburg Academy; the sale of his property in Pennsylvania; the purchase of the Hampton rights belonging to his brother and sisters; his marriage in July 1936, to Alice Lucas, his childhood sweetheart and sister of his first teacher, Miss Annie Ashburn Lucas; and finally the "return." He wrote his son Irv, "...Hampton forever is ours. It would finish me to sell the place...."

Unable to contain her joy at his plan to come back to Hampton, Sue Alston wrote this letter to Archibald:

R.F.D. 1. Box. 93.
Santee. S.C.
Oct. 25. 1937.

Dear Mr. Arch,

I just write you and miss Alice to know that Everything is surprise to me....I ever did think that you was a smartt man but not that smartt. Tis a good thing that the Lord is all man maker and is a good thing that he blessin it and I am proud that the old place fixing up....one thing is on my mind I want to know how can you keep a brave heart always....you had made this place here real pretty what I mean real pretty and I know that I can Raise chickens and Raise my Garden and that will be a Joyful thing for me and I am very proud of this place you don't know but the Lord know....

Sue Alston

All of Hampton would soon rejoice—Archibald wrote Irvine October 27, 1937:

Dear Irv,
....I am very busy packing up, speaking, & writing.
All's well here.
A month from now you and I will be livin'.
On the opposite page are inscriptions for the Hampton gates.

Your devoted,

Entering

Whatever brings you to this gate,
Whate'er the place from which you come,
In human kind's wide fellowship,
Be welcome to this ancient Home.

Leaving

Whatever brought you to this gate,
In peace and joy and love, depart.
And may your life illumined be
By dreams of Hampton in your heart.

By the time Archibald had been "home" a year, his oldest son Arch, Jr., sent him a poem with his description of the new scene at Hampton.

Courtesy—Eleanor Stevenson Rutledge, Jacksonville, Alabama

Archibald Rutledge, Jr., on horseback at Hampton Plantation.

Rutledge Wildlife Enterprises
Nature Specialties

Arch Rutledge, Jr.
Negley Bldg.
Hagerstown

The old home has a new Master.
The cold hearth has a warm fire.
Great whispering pines
Chant melodic rhymes
To welcome once more the ancient glad times.
All *Hampton* is happy again.

Flintlock is back on the delta.
At long last the pinelands awake.
A gaunt slumbering bound
A great stag has found;
Challenging horns from the sunrise resound.
All *Hampton* is happy again.

So, here's to old *Hampton's new Master,*
Who has turned back the tide of the years.
Reborn are old dreams;
Restored are old streams;
Old stars are shining with brighter new beams.
All *Hampton* is happy again.

Affectionately
A.R. Jr.
11/22/38

To the joy of family and friends Archibald wrote of his experiences in restoring Hampton in one of his most popular works, *Home by the River,* which was published in three editions before his death. His writing created a mystical aura about Hampton with each revelation of hidden treasures, secret passages, and long-concealed nuggets of information. To his readers he epitomized all the "glory" of southern aristocracy as he delved into his own past and that of his ancestors. This gracious gentleman, who was fond of rising early and gathering dew-sprinkled bouquets of wild flowers for his wife, his daughter-in-law Eleanor, and for Hampton's guardian angel Sue Alston, became a part of his own legend. His reverence for the plantation and for the many generations of his family that had lived there, plus his genuine happiness at returning, seemed to kindle a spirit of gratitude within the poet. He considered himself only a privileged visitor, but for the next thirty years his invitation to his readers in *Home by the River,* "Strangers are welcome...I like them to come," was accepted by people from all over the world—visitors who were more than eager to be welcomed as guests, to be treated as family, and to be called "cousin" by the poet/owner of Hampton Plantation.

Epilogue

THE LEGEND

Hampton Plantation (1730–)

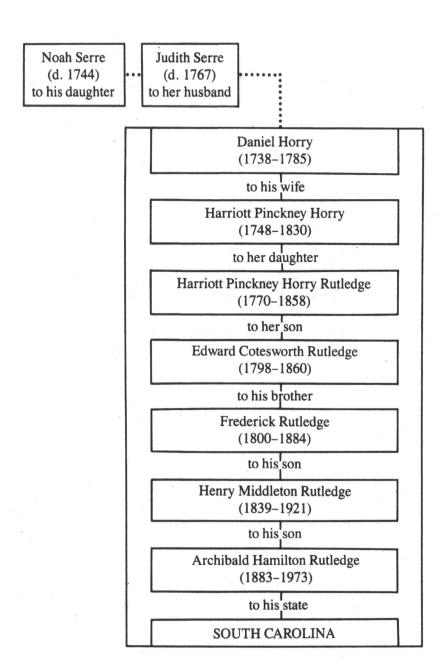

Noah Serre
(d. 1744)
to his daughter

Judith Serre
(d. 1767)
to her husband

Daniel Horry
(1738–1785)

to his wife

Harriott Pinckney Horry
(1748–1830)

to her daughter

Harriott Pinckney Horry Rutledge
(1770–1858)

to her son

Edward Cotesworth Rutledge
(1798–1860)

to his brother

Frederick Rutledge
(1800–1884)

to his son

Henry Middleton Rutledge
(1839–1921)

to his son

Archibald Hamilton Rutledge
(1883–1973)

to his state

SOUTH CAROLINA

Ownership—The Legend
Hampton Plantation
(1730–   )

Epilogue

The final chapter in the life of Hampton Plantation is still to be written. One era ended in 1971 when Archibald Rutledge sold the house and 275 acres to the state of South Carolina, but another is only now opening up.

As the last family member to own this proud and gracious stately mansion, with a mystique of its own harking back to the beginnings of the South and of the nation, he felt responsible for preserving not only the home of his ancestors but the warm aura of hospitality associated with the Rutledge domain. His years of residence were not necessarily easy but they were productive, as evidence by his voluminous writings. The literary world recognized his contributions with critical acclaim and his readers elevated his Hampton stories to a place of almost legendary importance. He could claim authorship of more books than any other South Carolinian, and his exceptional talents as a speaker made him popular with audiences across the country.

His sons were proud of their father, whom they fondly called "Flintlock," and the father highly regarded each of his sons as an individual personality. His oldest son, Henry Middleton, "Mid," attended Mercersburg College, graduated from Princeton University in 1932, and pursued the study of medicine at Johns Hopkins and the Medical College of Charleston, interned at West Baltimore General Hospital, and opened his own clinic in 1940 in Laurens, South Carolina. However, three years later he was critically injured in an accident and died January 18, 1943.

The other two sons were in World War II military service at that time, Arch, Jr., with the Navy in Africa and Irvine (Irv) with the United States legal staff in Cologne, Germany, as a non-combatant. Irv had followed Mid's pattern of studying first at Mercersburg, then earning an undergraduate degree from Princeton. He graduated from George Washington Law School in 1936, began law practice in Hagerstown, Maryland, in 1938, and took office as Associate Judge, 4th Judicial Circuit of Maryland, on January 4, 1962. Following World War II Arch, Jr., settled at Hampton, pursued work in several areas of conservation, wrote poems and a wildlife column, and with his wife Eleanor (m. 1942) helped his father manage Hampton.

By 1946 Eleanor Stevenson Rutledge was serving as hostess to the hundreds of yearly visitors eager to meet her father-in-law and person-

Hampton Plantation (1948).

Archibald Rutledge, Jr. and his wife, Eleanor Stevenson Rutledge, standing in front of the old kitchen at Hampton (1948).

Visiting "cousins" from Alabama—left to right: Horace Lee Stevenson, Katherine Sabina Stevenson, Archibald Rutledge, John Forney Stevenson, Sarah Katherine Stevenson, and Margaret Segrest (1948).

ally experience the romance and nostalgia surrounding the Santee plantation. "Arch's Eleanor" continued "Miss Margaret's" tradition of Sunday school for the children of the plantation workers. Her grandmother (Septima Sexta Middleton Rutledge Forney) and her husband's grandfather (Colonel Henry Middleton Rutledge) were both grandchildren of Septima and Henry Rutledge of Nashville, Tennessee. For Eleanor and Arch their kinship and marriage brought together the pre-Revolutionary ties of the Middleton/Pinckney/Rutledge families so identified with Hampton's early history. It was only fitting, following the death of Arch, Jr., in 1959 that Eleanor remain at Hampton as hostess for her father-in-law whom she lovingly called "Dad."

Archibald Rutledge was injured by an automobile in 1967, his wife Alice died the following year, the family was scattered, and it was evident by then that Hampton's future needed to be considered. It was decided that the best course was to sell the house and some land to the state of South Carolina, a decision that would insure its careful protection and upkeep. A coincidental event occurred the same week that Archibald and his son Irvine decided to sell. The "Summer Place" in McClellanville, which had been out of the family for some time, was put on the market for sale. Irvine arranged for the purchase of his father's birthplace and Archibald moved there for his remaining years. He died September 15, 1973.

Recognizing Hampton as a unique national treasure, the state of South Carolina is now developing the plantation as a state park. Extensive restoration is underway to make it an interpretive museum so future generations can see and appreciate this legacy of the past, a true link with

Courtesy—Eleanor Stevenson Rutledge, Jacksonville, Alabama

Archibald Hamilton Rutledge and his second wife, Alice Lucas Rutledge.

Courtesy—South Carolina State Parks, Recreation, and Tourism, Columbia, South Carolina.

Interior window frames. Hampton Plantation.

Courtesy—South Carolina State Parks, Recreation, and Tourism, Columbia, South Carolina.

Former exterior cornice, later plastered over. Hampton Plantation.

events and people that comprise American history. Michael Foley, Ray Sigmon, and Marion Edmonds of the South Carolina Department of Parks, Recreation, and Tourism are responsible for executing the master plan of completion.

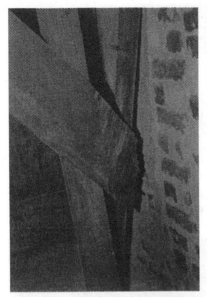

Courtesy—South Carolina State Parks, Recreation, and Tourism, Columbia, South Carolina

Courtesy—South Carolina State Parks, Recreation, and Tourism, Columbia, South Carolina.

Cut corner brace next to upstairs fireplace. Hampton Plantation.

Stencil pattern on wall. Hampton Plantation.

Visitors today, greeted by Ranger Bob Mitchell and by Will Alston, hear tales told of Hampton Plantation that embody the romance and imagination characteristic of all great manor houses in fact and fiction. Their inward eye see shadowy Sewee Indians, Huguenot settlers, fearsome coastal pirates. They explore the stairway and tunnel escape route of Francis Marion, the Swamp Fox of the Revolution. They admire the giant oak tree that George Washington saved. They see the room where the tragic suicide, John Henry Rutledge, died in 1830 and "hear tell" of the many visits his ghost has since made to his old haunts. They are shown the likely locations in the front lawn where family valuables are said to be buried as precautions against Sherman's raiders. They can look for the secret panel where Archibald found a map purported to locate these treasures. And finally, they look with awe at the closet floor where one caretaker, returning to the locked mansion after two week's absence, found a dew-laden bouquet of Hampton wildflowers, evidence that the spirit of Archibald Rutledge still hovers over his beloved home, bringing tributes today as he did in life.

And still keeping vigil over the proud estate is Sue Alston, whose memories recall over one hundred years of laughter and tears in her

Courtesy—Sarah Katherine Stevenson, Jacksonville, Alabama

Visitors from Alabama in front of the Washington
Oak at Hampton Plantation (1948).

Photo—Genon Hickerson Neblett

Will Alston still welcomes visitors to Hampton
Plantation.

beloved home. In the past year she has had corrective eye surgery so that
her vision, once limited to the "shadow of my finger," now includes the
world outside her cabin, the faces of "my people I had in Hampton" who
visit as often as possible, and her "ladies from Tennessee" who were
inspired by her joy and courage to capture in words "that great day in
Hampton" for all the generations yet to come.

Hidden Glory is a biography of a house, and with it the story of our
nation, particularly of our South, and of the people who lived in it and
loved it and helped make this nation what it is today. *Hidden Glory* is
designed to extend Archibald Rutledge's invitation to walk under the
Washington oak, just past the edge of recorded history, onto the portico
of his "home by the river" and to listen with him to the voices that whis-
per of Hampton, the legend of the South Santee.

APPENDICES

Photo—Jim Wheeler
Courtesy—Owner, Richard Goddard,
Nashville, Tennessee

Portion of Rose Hill, home of Septima and Henry Rutledge, which remains at the corner of Rutledge and Lea streets, Nashville, Tennessee.

Photo—Jim Wheeler

Rutledge plot, Old City Cemetery—Nashville, Tennessee.

Courtesy—Henderson/Ward Agency, Nashville, Tennessee

Home of William B. and Emma Fredericka "Minna" Rutledge Reese at 42 Rutledge Street—built c. 1873, renovated 1981 by William F. Henderson and David L. Ward as offices for their advertising agency. The Reese home is on the National Register of Historic Sites and received an award of merit from the Metropolitan Historic Commission of Nashville.

Appendix A

Guide to Areas Mentioned in *Hidden Glory*

Many of the areas mentioned in *Hidden Glory* may be visited today. In Nashville, Tennessee, is the Rutledge Hill area, the city's first subdivision, and a portion of Rose Hill remains, owned by Richard Goddard. The Minna Rutledge Reese home has been revitalized as headquarters for the Henderson/Ward agency—Rutledge Public Relations. The Old City Cemetery is nearby as is the former University of Nashville campus. Along the Elk River in Tennessee's Franklin and Coffee counties is the site of Chilhowee, which is no longer standing, but the Sherrill family points out for visitors the foundation stones, the millrace, and the slave burial plot.

In Jacksonville, Alabama, the Forney-Stevenson home, owned by Eleanor Stevenson Rutledge and Mary Stevenson Poling, and the Magnolias, owned by the estate of Annie Rowan Forney Daugette, are usually open to the public once a year under auspices of the Jacksonville Heritage Association.

In Fletcher, North Carolina, The Meadows and Calvary Episcopal Church and cemetery are constant reminders of the Blake family's role in the establishment of that community. In nearby Flat Rock are the Rutledge Cottage, owned by Mr. and Mrs. Alexander Schenck; Brookland, with its substantial two-story house built in 1836 for Charles Edmondston, wealthy Charleston businessman, and "Fred's place," built by Frederick Rutledge in 1829 both now owned by Mr. and Mrs. Gene Staton; and St. John in the Wilderness Episcopal Church. All are still a viable part of the "little-Charleston-of-the-mountains."

In Greenville, South Carolina, there remain Governor Henry Middleton's home, Whitehall, and Christ Episcopal Church. In Columbia is the governor's mansion and the State House. In Camden, is Bethesda Presbyterian Church where Lafayette preached the funeral oration for his fellow-officer Baron de Kalb.

The entire city of Charleston, with its restored homes, churches, and public buildings, takes its place in Hampton's story. Of special interest is the building of the Church of the Redeemer, erected in 1916 at the corner of Market and East Bay Streets. The land it is on was donated in 1853 by Harriott Pinckney, daughter of Charles Cotesworth Pinckney, to be held

Photo—Genon Hickerson Neblett

Eleanor Stevenson Rutledge
(Mrs. Archibald Rutledge, Jr.)—
longtime hostess at Hampton
Plantation, now of Jacksonville,
Alabama.

in trust until a church for seamen could be built. It now houses one of
Charleston's finest restaurants.

Outside Charleston on Highway 61, the visitor is beckoned to step
into the past at Middleton Place House and Gardens. A registered National Historic Landmark, Middleton Place is owned by Charles H.P.
Duell and features the first formal gardens laid out in America. The
house was burned by Sherman's troops in 1865 and was crumbled during
the earthquake of 1886 so only the south flanker remains. This portion is
a museum under the aegis of Middleton Place Foundation with Sarah
Lytle as director. In McClellanville the "Summer Place" is still the va-
cation home of Judge Irvine Rutledge.

Appendix B

Hampton Plantation

Shrimp Pilau

1 cup celery—chopped
$^1/_2$ cup green pepper—chopped
1 large onion—chopped
3 tablespoons butter
1 cup rice (raw)
2 cups chicken stock
or chicken bouillon
salt and pepper to taste
dash of ground red pepper
1 teaspoon curry powder
1 teaspoon Worcestershire sauce
1 hard cooked egg—chopped
1 (4 oz.) can pimento
2 cups boiled fresh shrimp

Brown the celery, green pepper, and onion in butter in a heavy skillet. Add rice and cook until rice is brown. Add chicken stock, salt, curry powder and Worcestershire sauce. Cover skillet and cook until rice is fluffy. Add egg, pimento, and shrimp.

—Courtesy of:
Eleanor Stevenson Rutledge
Sabina Stevenson Guyton

Appendix C

Books by Archibald Rutledge, with copyright dates and dedications

Under the Pines, 1906. (Father)
Banners of the Coast, 1908. (Florence Hart Rutledge)
The Spirit of Mercersburg, 1909.
New Poems, 1915. (Camille Hart Irvine)
Tom and I on the Old Plantation, 1918. (Tom Rutledge)
Songs from a Valley, 1919. (Three sisters)
Plantation Game Trails, 1921. (Three sons)
Old Plantation Days, 1921. (William Mann Irvine)
South of Richmond, 1923. (Hart)
Days Off in Dixie, 1924. English, 1925. (J. Earlston Thropp, Jr.)
Heart of the South, 1924. (Irvine)
Collected Poems, 1925. (Florence Hart Rutledge)
Children of Swamp and Woods, 1927. (Camilla, Scott, Pinckney)
Life's Extras, 1928. (Florence)
Peace in the Heart, 1930. (James C. Derieux)
Bolio and Other Dogs, 1930.
Flower of Hope, 1930.
Wild Life of the South, 1935. (Prince Alston)
When Boys Go Off to School, 1935.
Heart's Quest, 1936. (Ann Ashburn Lucas)
Brimming Chalice, 1936. (Flora McDonald and Margaret Kingsley Rutledge)
An American Hunter, 1937. (Three sons)
My Colonel and His Lady, 1937. (Alice)
The Sonnets, 1938.
It Will Be Daybreak Soon, 1938.
Rain on the Marsh, 1940.
Home by the River, 1941, 1955, 1960.
Love's Meaning, 1943. (HMR IV)
Christ Is God, 1944. (the Rev. Alexander Mitchell)
Hunter's Choice, 1946. (HMR IV)
God's Children, 1947. (Eleanor)

Beauty of the Night, 1947.
The Angel Standing, 1948. (Eugene and Jane Burden)
The Everlasting Light, 1949.
A Wildwood Tale, 1950.
Heart's Citadel, 1953. (Jo, Joey, Jean)
Beauty in the Heart, 1953. (Holley and Lyons)
Brimming Tide, 1954.
Those Were the Days, 1955. (Elise and Donald Rutledge)
Santee Paradise, 1956.
From the Hills to the Sea, 1958. (Ann, Avery, Joan Rockefeller)
Deep River, 1960, 1966. (Jo Aldrich Harris)
World Around Hampton, 1960. (Garla and Jean)
Ballad of the Howling Hound, 1962. (AHR, Jr.)
Willie Was a Lady, c1966. (Dorothy Gaston)
How Wild Was My Village, 1969.
The Woods and Wild Things I Remember, 1970. (Dorothy Gaston)
Poems in Honor of S. C. Tricentennial, 1970.
I Hear America Singing, 1970. (Ann Rockefeller)
Bright Angel, n.d.

Appendix D

Prose Works of Archibald Rutledge

Housed in the South Caroliniana Library

(These are primarily feature articles, short stories, and editorials. Some became chapters of books, many overlap each other, and others are incomplete. Most of the items are in manuscript; some are tearsheets.)

(accidental shots)
"Acts in Emergencies"
"Adventures with the
  Black Prince"
"Alas for Theodosia"
(alligator, bull)
"Along Nature's Trail"
"Amateur Archeologists"
"An Amateur Trapper"
"Antiquity Is Looking at Me"
"Are Hunters Cruel?"
"Assassin!"
"Babes on Their Mother's
  Breast"
"The Baffling Bald Mountains"
"Ballad of the Howling Hound"
"Banded Death"
"Barba Amarilla"
"The Battle of King's Mountain"
"Be Very Courageous"
"Beautiful Wings"
(beauty, real)
"Behind the Veil"
"Benbow's Nose"
"Better Baseball"
"Bible Stories Retold"
"Birds and Ricefields"
"Birds Give Us Wings"
"Birthright and the Pottage"

"The Bishop Earns a Gobbler"
"Black and White Eagles"
"The Black Avenger"
"The Black Buck of Hampton"
"The Black Pileated"
"The Blessings of Insecurity"
(boar, trapping a)
"The Bohun Word"
"Bonnie and Rip"
"Born to Be Brave"
"Born to Danger"
"Boyhood in a Rice Field"
(boys, teaching)
"Boys Will Be Boys"
"Bridges of the Woodmont"
"Bright College Years"
"Buck at the Secret Crossing"
"Buck in the Rain"
"Bucks Don't Want to Be
  Trophies"
"Bugle"
"Burial of the Guns"
"But He Is a Turkey Hunter"
"Case of the Howling Hound"
"The Champion"
"A Change of Heart"
(Cherokee folklore)
"Cherokee Princess"
"Children of the Night"

"Christmas Angel"
"A Christmas Hunt"
"A Christmas Story"
"Circumventing Trouble"
(civil rights)
"A Civil War Romance"
"Close Calls in the Wild"
"A Closer Look at the White
    Tail"
"Combat in the Wild"
"A Commando of the Mountains"
(conference address)
"Consider the Nest"
"The Contagion of Valor"
"A Critical Hunting Moment"
"Croatan"
"Cumberland Valley Memories"
"Daft Katie"
"Dangerous Beasts"
"Dangerous Beauty"
"Darkness and the Light"
"The Deer and the Hound"
(deer food)
"Deer of the Coastal Island"
(deer stories)
(deer, a three-legged)
"Demon of the Ocean"
"Demons of the Delta"
"The Dilemma of the Wild"
"Disappearing Historic Jewels"
"The Dog That Saw Death"
"Dogs I Have Known"
(dogs, wild)
"Don't Lose Your Nerve"
"A Dragon of the Prime"
"Dramatic Encounters in the
    Wild"
(ducks)
"Early Adventures"
"Earth Our Mother"

"The End of the Hunt"
"The Enemies of Quail"
"Enemies of the Wild Duck"
(English writers)
"Eric"
"Etiquette Among the Beasts"
"Every One His Own Physician"
(exceptions in nature)
"The Faith of a Naturalist"
"Falkland Island Battle"
"Fancy Meeting You Here!"
"Feathered Funsters"
"The Fish Weren't Biting"
(Fitzgerald, Georgia)
"Flat As a Paddle"
"Flora's Buck"
(flowers)
"The Four Wetzels"
"Frater Niger, Quo Vadis"
"Genevieve Finishes"
"Gentleman from Oshkosh"
"Getting Grace on the
    Streamliner"
"Ghost Point Buck"
"Gil-obble"
"God's Gleaners"
"Golden Barrier"
"The Golden Robber"
"Gospel Music"
"The Great American Public"
"The Great Collecting Game"
"The Great Gobbler of Path
    Valley"
"The Great King"
"Great Misses"
"Great Mistakes"
"The Great River"
"A Great Wild Boar"
"Grouse of the Little Hills"
"Guning Goofs"

(Mobile Jones)
"Mobile's Champion"
"Monarch of the Sky"
"Monarchs of the River Swamps"
"A Monster"
"A Monster's Nest"
"Monsters of the Swamp"
"The Most Dangerous Animal
  to Hunt"
"Mothers of the Wilds"
"Motto for Parents"
"My Christmas Woods"
"My Colonel"
"My Colonel's Lady"
"My Colonel's Last Hunt"
"My Craziest Turkey Hunt"
"My Favorite Hunting Story"
"My Favorite Tree"
"My Gobbler"
"My Heroines"
"My Last Grouse Hunt"
"My Life as a Hunter"
"My Little Lakes"
"My Memories of Rachel Carson"
"My Most Memorable Deer Hunt"
"My Most Memorable Dog"
"My Narrowest Escapes"
"My Wild Azaleas"
"My Winter Woods"
"Mysteries of Nature"
"The Mystery of Charm"
"Mystery of the Honey Guide"
"Mystery of the Lost Island"
"Nacht und Nebel"
"Naivete and Courtship"
"The Native Returns"
"The Nature of God"
"Nature on the Offbeat"
"Nature Says It with Flowers"
"Nature's Children Use Their Hands"

"Nature's Flying Engineers"
"Nature's Guarded Secrets"
"Nature's Masterpiece"
"Nature's Navigators"
"Nature's Outlaws"
"Nature's Trail Blazers"
"Negro Woodsmen I Have Known"
"A Nice Arrangement"
(night)
"Night Is in the Pinelands"
"Noblesse Oblige"
"Not All Yet known"
"Not to the Victor"
"Notes on the Swallow-Tailed
  Kite"
"Nothing Ever Happens Here"
"Oak of the Golden Cup"
"October's Mad Moon"
"Of Human Dignity"
"Old Plantation Days"
"The Old Plantations Live
  again"
"The Olympics: Two Misgivings"
"Only One Captain"
"Oolalee's Rival"
"An Ordinary Christmas"
"Our Changing Wildlife"
"Our Gobbler"
"Our Heritage of the Oaks"
"Painter and the Pioneer"
"Patsy and the Princess"
"Peace through Tolerance"
"Peerless Cinchona"
"People Can't Stand Affection"
"Perils of a Woodsman"
"Personal Conservation"
"A Pioneer Hunter"
"The Pirates' Chests"
"A Plantation Boyhood"
"A Plantation Christmas"

"Their Baffling Maneuvers"
"Their One Great Mistake"
"They Change Their Habits"
"They Live Alone and Like It"
"They May Change Their Ways"
"They Put You on the Spot"
"They Quite Outdo Me"
"They're Wise to Us"
"The Thing in the Tomb
   of Raven McCloud"
"Think on These Things"
"Thinking Your Way"
"The Third Murderer of Macbeth"
"Those Bearded Men"
"Those Big Mountain Boys"
"Those Were the Days"
"Tiger! Tiger!"
"Titania Herself"
"Trailing Hound"
"The Treasures of Darkness"
"Two Needles in a Haystack"
"The Triumph of the Spirit"
"Trophy of a Lifetime"
(trouble, compensations of)
"The Trout of Dickey's Run"
"True Stories of the Civil War"
"Two Famous Rubies"
"Tyler Somerset's Somersault"
"Unanswered Questions"
"Under the Greenwood Tree"
"Unexpected Company"
"Unforgettable Character"
"A Universal Source of Joy"
"Valor in the Wilds"
"The Vanishing Pegram"
"War Is Not Always Just Killing"
"A Wary Stag"
(water creatures)
"The Ways of the Wild Gobbler"
"What Every Hunter Knows"

"What Happened to Poetry?"
"What I Have Learned About
   Training Dogs"
"What New Religion?"
"What of Our Gold"
"What Teachers Learn"
"What Your Buck May Do"
"When Boys Go Off to School"
"When the Yankee Band Played Dixie"
"When Washington Visited
   My Home"
"Where Have They Gone?"
"White Shark"
"Who Buried the Treasure"
"Who Knows Nature Best?"
"Why Did I Miss?"
"Why I Disbelieve Darwin"
"Why I Envy Wild Things"
"Why I Taught My Boys To Be
   Hunters"
"Wild Asters"
"Wild Boars"
"Wild Brother As an Engineer"
"Wild Brother Winters Through"
"Wild Brotherhood"
"Wild Courtship"
"Wild Fugitives"
"Wild Game and Civilization"
"Wild Genius"
"Wild Sentinels"
"Wild Songsters"
"Wild Things at Play"
"Wild Turkey Stalking"
"Wild Turkey's"
"Wild Turkeys in Pennsylvania
   Fifty Years Ago"
(wild wisdom)
"Wilderness Defiling"
"Wilderness Hunter: Meshach
   Browning"

"Wildlife in a Flood"
"Wildlife in Repose"
"Wildlife Is Rugged"
"Wildlife Safety Zones"
"Wildlife in the South"
"Wildlife's Athletic Champions"
"A Wildwood Christmas"
"Wildwood Majesty"
"Wingshooting by the Sea"

"Women and Children First"
"Wonder"
"Wood Duck's Nest"
"Woodpecker's Home"
"The World Around Hampton"
"The Wrong Gobbler"
"Yellow and a Yard Wide"
"You Take Her"

Appendix E

Additional Collection of Magazine Articles by Archibald Rutledge Housed in the South Caroliniana Library

"An Adventurous Day." *Field and Stream,* July 1944.

"All of a Misty Morning." *Field and Stream,* November 1921.

"Big Tom." *Field and Stream,* November 1931.

"Big Tom's in Big Timber." *Field and Stream,* March 1927.

"Blue's Buck." *Field and Stream,* January 1939.

"Breaking in on a Banquet." *Field and Stream,* June 1923.

"Brook Trout on Minnows." *Field and Stream,* April 1926.

"The Buck with the Palmated Horns." *Field and Stream,* December 1941.

"Bucks Are Like That." *Field and Stream,* July 1938.

"Certain Great Stags." *Field and Stream,* October 1927.

"Chance Shots." *Field and Stream,* January 1927.

"Christmas Eve Buck." *Field and Stream,* December 1929.

"Critical Momemts." *Field and Stream,* October 1945.

"Dangerous Beasts." *Field and Stream,* May 1940.

"Danny Knows His Ducks." *Field and Stream,* February 1935.

"A Day in the Pineland Wilds." *Field and Stream,* April 1921.

"Daybreak in the Ocean." *Field and Stream,* February 1936.

"The Ducks at Tranquility." *Field and Stream,* May 1927.

"Encounters with the Diamondback." *Field and Stream,* September 1923.

"The Fall of the Emperor." *Field and Stream,* September 1935.

"Game I've Given Away." *Field and Stream,* September 1944.

"Gentlemen, the King!." *Field and Stream,* November 1944.

"Give It to the Big Bird." *Field and Stream,* November 1924.

"Gobbler of Lone Pine Ridge." *Field and Stream,* December 1930.

"The Great Bird Comes Back." *Field and Stream,* December 1926.

"Grouse of the Cloudlands." *Field and Stream,* March 1933.

"The Horn Architecture of the White Tail." *Field and Stream,* December 1927.

"Horns on the Delta." *Sports Afield,* September 1938.

"A Hunt at the Kinlock Club." *Outdoor Life,* March 1934.

"A Hunt with the Oakland Pack." *Field and Stream,* ?.

"The Hunter and the Law." *Field and Stream*, September 1930.

"I'm Listening for You." *Field and Stream*, November 1942.

"Invading the Sanctuaries." *Field and Stream*, March 1936.

"It's the Scotch in Them." *Field and Stream*, February 1939.

"Joel and the Marsh-Buck." *Field and Stream*, February 1921.

"The Lady in Green." *Field and Stream*, October 1941.

"Last Chances." *Field and Stream*, January 1937.

"Man, Aren't They Different!" *Field and Stream*, August 1944.

"Master Minds." *Field and Stream*, April 1927.

"Milstead Ropes One." *Field and Stream*, March 1926.

"Miss Seduction Struts Her Stuff." *Field and Stream*, January 1934.

"The Most Unforgettable Character I've Met (Prince Alston)." *Reader's Digest*, November 1943.

"My Greatest Thrill." *Field and Stream*, August 1930.

"My Twilight Buck." *Field and Stream*, September 1924.

"Notes on Hunting Horns." *Field and Stream*, October 1921.

"Odyssey of Old Clubfoot, Part I." *Field and Stream*, September 1928.

"Odyssey of Old Clubfoot, Part II." *Field and Stream*, October 1928.

"Oh These Hunters." *Sports Afield*, October 1941.

"Pauper Princess." *Outdoor Life*, August 1938.

"Poinsetta and Sparkplug." *Field and Stream*, October 1922.

"Prince of the Swampland." *Field and Stream*, July 1930.

"The Prince of the Woodlands." *Outdoor Life*, January 1934.

"The Quail of the Kalmias." *Field and Stream*, November 1933.

"Radio of the Wild." *Outdoor Life*, January 1932.

"Rainbows in My Maryland." *Outdoor Life*, June 1934.

"Random Shots." *Outdoor Life*.

"Rattling Tails." *Field and Stream*, March 1928.

"Riding Them Up." *Field and Stream*, August 1931.

"Rifle or Shotgun for Deer." *Field and Stream*, September 1940.

"Snipe of the Pinelands." *Field and Stream*, February 1931.

"Some Startling Dogs." *Outdoor Life*, August 1932.

"Sometimes It Happens." *Field and Stream*, ?.

"A Stalk on the Dunes." *Field and Stream*, September 1934.

"Stalking Game." *Outdoor Life*, June 1944.

"Stalking Your Buck." *Outdoor Life*, December 1934.

"Steve Takes a Holiday." *Field and Stream*, January 1935.

"Tall Man of the Twilight." *Field and Stream*, March 1939.

"That Day at Dan's." *Field and Stream*, November 1925.

"They Love the Sources." *Field and Stream*, September 1923.

"This Happened to Me." *Outdoor Life*, September 1942.

"Those Fast Five Minutes." *Field and Stream*, March 1925.

"Was I Surprised!" *Outdoor Life*, August 1942.

"The Ways of the Wood Duck." *Field and Stream*, May 1919.

"Weather Makes the Hunting." *Outdoor Life*, January 1936.

"Well I'll Be Darned." *Field and Stream*, March 1922.

"What Every Deer Hunter Should Know." *Outdoor Life*, August 1946.

"What Scares Game." *Field and Stream*, October 1934.

"When Wambaw Bass Were Biting." *Field and Stream*, December 1923.

"Wild Life in a Drought." *Outdoor Life*, November 1930.

"The Woods Are Full of Danger." *Outdoor Life*, March 1944.

"You Can't Put Out the Sun." *American Magazine*, July 1932.

Resources

Historical societies, libraries, archives, foundations, private collections, and church registries all contain invaluable primary source material. Yet without the assistance of dedicated personnel, avid local historians, and those descendants and family members gracious enough to share their homes, their memories, and themselves the information for this biography would not have been complete. Grateful acknowledgment is given to the following:

Alabama
Gadsden;
Colonel Clarence W.
   Daugette, Jr.
Florence Throckmorton
   Daugette
Marcella Lawley
Jacksonville;
The Forney-Stevenson Home
   Mary Abernathy Stevenson
      Poling
   Eleanor Stevenson Rutledge
General John H. Forney
   Historical Society
General John H. Forney
   Chapter,
      United Daughters of the
      Confederacy
Jacksonville Heritage Association
The Magnolias
   Kathleen Daugette Carson
   Maurice Johnson
   Lenora Carr Murphree
Sarah Katherine Stevenson
Wren's Nest Gallery
   Larry Martin
   Crystal Hancock

Florida
Dunedin;
   Caroline Forney Gustafson

Georgia
Atlanta;
   Georgia State Archives
   Georgia Historical Society
Savannah;
   Margaret Hamilton Seabrook
   Harriott Rutledge Seabrook

Kentucky
Bowling Green;
The Kentucky Library
   Nancy Baird
   Elaine Harrison
Louisville;
The Filson Club
   Nellie Watson

Maryland;
Hagerstown;
   Judge & Mrs. Irvine Hart
      Rutledge

Mississippi
Pass Christian;
   Mrs. Philip St. George
      Ambler

New York
Saratoga Springs;
Office of City Historian
   Mrs. Michael E. Sweeney
   Larry Stone

North Carolina

Asheville;
    Mr. & Mrs. W.G. Hutchison
    Mr. & Mrs. Frederick
    Rutledge
Flat Rock;
Historic Flat Rock, Inc.
    John Wesley Jones
    Mrs. Robert E. Mason
The Old Mill
    Mr. & Mrs. Manus
Rutledge Cottage
    Mr. & Mrs. Alexander Schenck
St. John in the Wilderness
  Episcopal Church
    The Rev. Walter D. Roberts
    Mr. & Mrs. William I.
    Van Gelder
Elinor Gorham
Elizabeth Lowndes
Mr. & Mrs. Richard I'On
  Lowndes III
Elise Pinckney
Mr. & Mrs. Gene Staton
Fletcher;
Calvry Episcopal Church
The Meadows
    Mr. & Mrs. William T. Justice
    John C. Youngblood, Sr.
    Kellwood Company
Hendersonville;
The Times-News
Lucille S. Ray

Pennsylvania

Philadelphia;
Pennsylvania Historical Society
    James E. Mooney
    Lucy L. Hrivnak
    Diane Telian
Pittsburgh;
    Harriet P. Phillips

South Carolina

Camden;
Bethesda Presbyterian Church

Mrs. Frederick Reeves Rutledge
Charleston;
The Huguenot Society
  of South Carolina
    Martha B. Burns
Middleton Place Foundation
    Charles H. P. Duell
    Sarah Lytle
    Barbara Doyle
    R. Alan Powell
    Ann Suttle
South Carolina Historical
  Society
    Elise Pinckney
Isabella Leland
Kathryn Felder Stewart
Columbia;
State House of South Carolina
South Carolina House
  of Representatives
Sergeant-at-Arms Padgett
South Carolina State Department
  of Parks, Recreation, and
  Tourism-State Parks
    Marion Edmonds
    Michael Foley
    Ray Sigmon
South Carolina State
  Governor's Mansion
    Joan Davis
South Carolina State
  Library and Archives
University of South Carolina
    South Caroliniana Library
    Les Inabinett
    Charles Gay
    Allen Stokes
    Emily Carter
Silvia Sullivan
Greenville;
Christ Episcopal Church
Whitehall
Mr. & Mrs. David Hickerson
McClellanville;
Hampton Plantation
    Bob Mitchell
    Samuel Alston

Sue Alston
  Will Alston
The "Summer Place"
  Judge & Mrs. Irvine Hart
  Rutledge
St. James Santee Episcopal
  Church
Thames family
Mount Pleasant;
  Mr. & Mrs. Arch Guyton
  Mrs. & Mrs. Benjamin
  Bosworth Smith
Summerville;
  Douglas M. Crutchfield

Tennessee

Estill Springs;
  Mr. & Mrs. Richard I'On
  Lowndes III
Nashville;
Christ Episcopal Church
  Archives
  Laura Drake
Old City Cemetery
  Edythe Rucker Whitley
The Hermitage
  Ladies' Hermitage
  Association
  Edith Thornton
Public Library of Nashville
  and Davidson County
  Ben West Library

Dorothy Dale
Nashville Room
  Mary Glenn Hearne
  Hershel G. Payne
  Elsie Kolar
Rutledge Hill
Rose Hill
  Richard Goddard
Rutledge Public Relations
  Bill Henderson
  David Ward
Tennessee Historical Society
  James A. Hoobler
Tennessee State Library
  and Archives
  Chaddra Moore
  Leslie Pritikin
  John Thweatt
Frances Cate Grigsby
Mrs. Arthur Tatum
Rutledge Hill Community'
  Arthur Sherrill family
Sewanee;
University of the South
  Trudy Mignery
Winchester;
Franklin County Historical
  Society
Old Jail Museum
  Maye Gattis
Franklin County Library and
  Archives
  Nelle Hanson

Selected Bibliography

Abernthy, Thomas Perkins. *From Frontier to Plantation in Tennessee: A Study in Frontier Democracy.* Chapel Hill: The University of North Carolina Press, 1932.

Arnow, Harriette Simpson, *Flowering of the Cumberland.* New York: The Macmillan Company, 1963.

_____. *Seedtime on the Cumberland.* New York: The Macmillan Company, 1960.

Ball, William Watts. The State That Forgot: South Carolina's Surrender to Democracy. Indianapolis: The Bobbs-Merrill Company, 1932.

Bassett, John Spencer, Ph.D. (ed.). *Correspondence of Andrew Jackson.* Vol. III, *1820-1828.* Washington, D.C.: Carnegie Institution, 1933.

Becker, Stephen (trans.) *Diary of My Travels in America,* by Louis-Phillippe, King of France, 1830-1848. New York: Delacorte Press, 1977.

Brandau, Roberta Sewell (ed.). *History of Homes and Gardens, of Tennessee.* Nashville: Parthenon Press, 1936.

Burt, Jesse C. *Nashville: Its Life and Times.* Nashville: Tennessee Book Company, 1959.

Cheves, Langdon, Esq. "Middleton of South Carolina." Vol. I, *South Carolina Historical and Genealogical Magazine,* 1900. Vol XX, 1919.

Clayton, W. W. *The History of Davidson County, Tennessee.* 1880. Reprint. Nashville: Charles Elder, 1971.

Coke, Fletch. *Christ Church.* Nashville: Williams Printing Company, 1979.

Crabb, Alfred Leland. *Nashville: Personality of a City.* Indianapolis—New York: The Bobbs-Merrill Co., Inc., 1960.

Crane, Sophie, and Paul Crane. *Tennessee Taproots.* Old Hickory: Earle-Shields, 1976.

Crawford, Lee Forney. *Forney Forever.* Birmingham: Commercial Printing Co., 1967.

Davidson, Donald. *The Tennessee, Frontier to Secession,* Rivers of America Series, Vol. 1. New York: Rinehart & Co., 1946.

_____. *The Tennessee, The New River: Civil War to TVA,* Rivers of America Series, Vol. 2. New York: Rinehart & Co., 1948.

Dykeman, Wilma. *The French Broad.* Knoxville: University of Tennessee Press, 1966.

Egerton, John. *Nashville: The Faces of Two Centuries (1780-1980).* Nashville: Nashville Magazine, 1979.

Engel, Beth Bland. *The Middleton Family (including Myddleton and Myddelton): records from Wales, England, Barbados, and the Southern United States.* Jesup: Press of the Jesup Sentinel, 1972.

Fitzpatrick, John C. (ed.). *The Diaries of George Washington: 1748-1799.* Vol IV (1789-1799). Boston and New York: Houghton Mifflin Company, 1925.

Fogg, Mary Middleton Rutledge. *Barrington's Elements of Natural Science comprising Hydrology, Geognosy, Geology, Meteorology, Botany, Zoology, and Anthropology.* Nashville: Graves, Marks & Co., 1858.

_____ . *A Biblical View of the Church Catechism in reference to Baptismal Responsibilities: elucidating, by numerous texts of scripture, the doctrines and principles of the Church, with a view to confirmation.* Nashville: Paul & Tavel, 1870.

Fraser, Charles. *A Charleston Sketchbook (ed.).* Alice R. Huger Smith. Charleston: Carolina Art Association, 1971.

_____ . *Reminiscences of Charleston.* Charleston: Garnier & Company, 1969.

Freeman, Douglas Southall. *George Washington: a Biography.* Vol. 6, *Patriot and President.* New York: C. Scribner's Sons, 1948-1957.

_____ . *George Washington: a Biography.* Vol. 7, *First in Peace.* New York: C. Scribner's Sons, 1948-1957.

Goodpasture, A. V., and W. R. Garrett. *History of Tennessee, It's People and Institutions.* Nashville: Brandon Printing Co., 1900.

Goodspeed (ed.) *History of Tennessee from the earliest times to the present; together with an historical and a biographical sketch of Cannon, Coffee, DeKalb, Warren and White Counties.* Chicago and Nashville: Goodspeed, firm, publishers, 1887.

_____ . *History of Tennessee from the earliest times to the present; together with an historical and a biographical sketch of Giles, Lincoln, Franklin and Moore Counties.* Chicago and Nashville: Goodspeed, firm, publishers, 1886.

Graham, Eleanor (ed.) *Nashville: A Short History and Selected Buildings.* Nashville: Historical Commission of Metropolitan Nashville-Davidson County, Tennessee, 1974.

Grisby, Frances Cate. "Mary Middleton Rutledge Fogg," *Seven Women of Nashville: Nashville's Fine Flavor of Feminity.* Nashville: Public Library of Nashville and Davidson County, 1974.

Grimshawe, Leming. *The Church of St. John in the Wilderness, 1836-1936.* [pamphlet], 1968.

Hale, William Thomas, and Dixon Merritt. *History of Tennessee and Tennesseans.* Chicago: Lewis Publishing Co., 1913.

Jenkins, Mark. *Calvary Church: First 100 Years.* Fletcher: Calvary Episcopal Church, 1959.

Kemble, Frances Anne. *Journal of a Residence On a Georgia Plantation in 1838-1839.* New York: The New American Library, Inc., 1975.

Leach, Frank Willing. *Genealogy of the Signers of the Declaration of Independence: original letters and summaries.* 53 vols. from 1885 to 1916.

_____ . Typewritten Copy of original manuscipts. John Calvert and Evelyn R. Dale (eds.). 20 vols., 1927.

Leiding, Harriette Kershaw. *Historic and Romantic Charleston.* Philadelphia: J. B. Lippincott Company, 1931.

Linton, Calvin D., Ph. D. (ed.). *The American Almanac: A Diary of America.* Nashville: Thomas Nelson, Inc., 1977.

MacKellar, William H. *Chuwalee: Chronicles of Franklin County, Tennessee.* Winchester: Franklin County Historical Society, 1973.

Malone, Dumas. *The Story of the Declaration of Independence.* New York: Oxford University Press, 1954.

Marsh, Kenneth, and Blanche Marsh. *Historic Flat Rock: Where The Old South Lingers.* Columbia: R. L. Bryan Company, 1972.

Michael, William. *The Declaration of Independence.* Washington: Government Printing Office, 1904.

Middleton, Alicia Hopton. *Life in Carolina and New England in the Nineteenth Century.* Bristol (R.I.): privately printed, 1929.

Molloy, Robert. *Charleston: A Gracious Heritage.* New York: D. Appleton-Century Company, Inc., 1947.

Moltke-Hansen, David, and Sallie Doscher (eds.). *South Carolina Historical Society Manuscript Guide.* Charleston: South Carolina Historical Society, 1979.

Morris, Eastin. *Tennessee Gazetteer 1834 and Matthew Rhea's Map of the State of Tennessee 1832,* eds. Robert M. McBride and Owen Meredith. Nashville: The Gazetteer Press, 1971.

Owens, Loulie Latimer. *Guide to the Archibald Hamilton Rutledge Papers: 1860-1970.* South Caroliniana Library; Columbia, South Carolina, 1972-1974.

Owsley, Harriet Chappel (ed.). *Guide to the Processed Manuscripts of the Tennessee Historical Society.* Nashville: Tennessee Historical Commission, Tennessee State Library and Archives, 1969.

Patton, Sadie Smathers. *The Story of Henderson County.* Spartanburg: The Reprint Company, 1976.

Pinckney, Elise (ed.). *The Letterbook of Eliza Lucas Pinckney: 1739-1762.* Chapel Hill: The University of North Carolina Press, 1972.

Rankin, Anne (ed.). *Christ Church Nashville: 1829-1929.* Nashville: Marshall and Bruce, 1929.

Ravenel, Mrs. St. Julien. *Charleston: The Place and the People.* New York: The MacMillan Co., 1929.

Ray, Lenoir. *Postmarks: A History of Henderson County, North Carolina (1787-1968).* Chicago: Adams Press, 1970.

Rhett, Robert Goodwyn. *Charleston: An Epic of Carolina.* Richmond: Garrett and Massie, Incorporated, 1940.

Rutledge, Archibald. *Beauty in the Heart: including Meet Archibald Rutledge* by Frank S. Mead. Westwood: Fleming H. Revell Co., 1953.

_____. *God's Children.* Indianapolis-New York: The Bobbs-Merrill Company, 1947.

_____. *Home by the River.* Indianapolis-New York: The Bobbs-Merril Company, 1941.

_____. *Life's Extras.* New York-Chicago: Fleming H. Revell Co., 1928.

_____. *My Colonel and His Lady.* Indianapolis-New York: The Bobbs-Merrill Company, 1937.

_____. *Peace in the Heart.* Garden City: Doubleday & Company, Inc., 1949.

Rutledge, Frederick: *Fairfields of Memory.* Asheville: Stephens Press, Inc., 1958.

Rutledge, Irvine Hart. *We Called Him Flintlock.* Columbia: The R. L. Bryan Co., 1974.

Rutledge, Sarah. *The Carolina Housewife* (ed.). Anna Wells Rutledge. Columbia: University of South Carolina Press, 1979.

Simms, William Gilmore. *The History of South Carolina, from its First European Discovery to its Erection into a Republic*. Redfield, 1860.

Stoney, Samuel Gaillard; Albert Simons; and Samuel Lapham, Jr. (eds.). *Plantations of the Carolina Low Country*. Charleston: Carolina Art Association, 1938.

Templin, Eleanor. "Franklin County Familes: The Remarkable Rutledge Family." *The Franklin County Historical Review*. Vol. VII, 1976.

Thomas, Jane H. *Old Days in Nashville. 1895-96*. Reprint. Nashville: Charles Elder, 1969.

Uhlendorf, Bernhard Alexander. *The Siege of Charleston*. New York: New York Times, 1968.

Waller, George. *Saratoga: Sage of an Impious Era*. Englewood Cliffs: Prentice Hall, Inc., 1966.

Webber, Mabel L. (ed.). "The Thomas Pinckney Family of South Carolina." *South Carolina Historical and Genealogical Magazine*. Vol. XXXIX, 1938.

_____ . "Dr. John Rutledge and His Descendants." *South Carolina Historical and Genealogical Magazine*. Vol. XXXI, 1930.

Wheeler, Mary Bray and Genon Hickerson Neblett. *Chosen Exile: The Life and Times of Septima Sexta Middleton Rutledge, American Cultural Pioneer*. 1980. Reprint. Nashville: Rutledge Hill Press, 1982.

Williams, Frances Leigh. *A Founding Family: The Pinckneys of South Carolina*. New York and London: Harcourt Brace Jovanovich, 1978.

Windrow, John E. (ed.). *Peabody and Alfred Leland Crabb: The Story of Peabody as Reflected in Selected Writings of Alfred Leland Crabb*. Nashville: Williams Press, 1977.

Wooldridge, John. *History of Nashville, Tennessee*. 1890. Reprint. Nashville: Charles Elder, 1970.

Index

www.ingramcontent.com/pod-product-compliance
Ingram Content Group UK Ltd.
Pitfield, Milton Keynes, MK11 3LW, UK
UKHW020816120325

456141UK00001B/97